India, Europe and Conflict Resolution in South Asia

India, Europe and Conflict Resolution in South Asia

Edited by
Rajendra K. Jain

Education and Culture
Lifelong Learning Programme
JEAN MONNET

KNOWLEDGE WORLD
KW Publishers Pvt Ltd
New Delhi

ISBN 978-93-83649-40-2

Published in India by Kalpana Shukla

KNOWLEDGE WORLD
KW Publishers Pvt Ltd
4676/21, First Floor, Ansari Road, Daryaganj, New Delhi 110002
Phone: +91 11 23263498/43528107
Email: knowledgeworld@vsnl.net • www.kwpub.com

2011 FPBA BEST PUBLISHERS AWARD (ENGLISH)

Printed and Bound in India

Contents

List of Abbreviations

ADB	Asian Development Bank
ANSF	Afghanistan National Security Forces
ASEAN	Association of South East Asian Nations
BIMSTEC	Bangladesh-India-Myanmar-Sri Lanka-Thailand Economic Cooperation
BJP	Bharatiya Janata Party
BSA	Bilateral Security Agreement
CFA	Ceasefire Agreement
CFSP	Common Foreign and Security Policy
CIDA	Canadian Development Agency
CSDP	Common Security and Defence Policy
CSOs	Civil Society Organizations
CSP	Country Strategy Paper
DFID	Department for International Development
DRC	Democratic Republic of Congo
EBA	Everything but Arms
EC	European Commission
EEC	European Economic Community
EIDHR	European Initiative for Democracy and Human Rights
ESDP	European Security and Defence Policy
ESS	European Security Strategy
ETA	Euskadi Ta Askatasuna or Basque Homeland and Freedom
EULEX	European Union Rule of Law Mission
EUPOL	European Police Mission in Afghanistan
GiZ	German Federal Enterprise for International Cooperation
GSP	Generalized System of Preferences
GOSL	Government of Sri Lanka
ICRC	International Committee of the Red Cross

IDPs	Internally Displaced Persons
IfS	Instrument for Stability
INGOs	International Non-governmental Organizations
IPKF	Indian Peace Keeping Force
ISAF	International Security Assistance Force
JCMB	Joint Coordination and Monitoring Board
KIO	Kachin Independence Organization
LDCs	Least Developed Countries
LEP	Look East Policy
LLRC	Lessons Learnt and Reconciliation Commission
LTTE	Liberation Tigers of Tamil Eelam
LoC	Line of Control
MIP	Multi-Annual National Indicative Programme
NATO	North Atlantic Treaty Organization
NCGUB	National Coalition Government of the Union of Burma
NGO	Non Governmental Organization
NLD	National League of Democracy
NSS	National Security Strategy
OHCHR	Office of the High Commission on Human Rights
OSCE	Organization for Security and Cooperation in Europe
P-TOMS	Post-Tsunami Operational Management Structure
PRSP	Poverty Reduction Strategy Papers
R2P	Responsibility to Protect
RMO	Risk Management Office
SAARC	South Asian Association for Regional Cooperation
SIPRI	Stockholm International Peace Research Institute
SLDG	Sri Lanka Donor Group
SLORC	State Law and Order Restoration Council
SLMM	Sri Lankan Monitoring Mission
SSR	Security Sector Reforms
UN	United Nations
UNDOF	UN Disengagement Observer Force
UNIFIL	United Nations Interim Force in Lebanon
UNSC	United Nations Security Council

Contributors

John Doyle is Director of the Institute for International Conflict Resolution and Reconstruction and Executive Dean of DCU Faculty of Humanities and Social Sciences. He was previously Head of the School of Law and Government and before that founding co-Director of the Centre for International Studies in Dublin City University. His research interests include comparative nationalist and ethnic conflict, Northern Ireland, conflict in South Asia and Irish foreign policy. He is Editor of *Irish Studies in International Affairs*.

Rajendra K. Jain is Director, Europe Area Studies Programme and Jean Monnet Chair, Centre for European Studies, Jawaharlal Nehru University, New Delhi and Adjunct Professor (Research), Monash European and EU Studies Centre, Monash University, Melbourne. He has been Visiting Professor at Freiburg, Leipzig and Tübingen universities in Germany, the Maison des Sciences de l'Homme, Paris and the Asia-Europe Institute, University of Malaya (2010). He was formerly Humboldt Fellow at the University of Constance and the School of Slavonic and East European Studies, University of London and Visiting International Fellow, Monash Europe and EU Centre, Melbourne (2009). He is the author/editor of over 30 books including the editor of *India and the European Union: Building a Strategic Partnership* (2007), *India and the European Union in a Changing World* (2014) and *Multiculturalism in India and Europe* (2014).

Patryk Kugiel is an analyst at the International Economic Relations and Global Issues Programme at the Polish Institute of International Affairs (PISM). He is a specialist on South Asia and international development cooperation. His research in PISM focuses on Indian and Pakistani foreign policies, security situation in South Asia, U.S. and EU policies towards the region, implications of India's rise on global order as well as development cooperation policy of Poland and the EU. He is the co-editor of *India-Poland Relations in the 21st Century: Vistas for Future Cooperation* (New Delhi: Vij Books, 2014).

Keerthi Sampath Kumar is an Erasmus Mundus PhD Scholar, Institute of International Relations, Warsaw University. She was formerly Research Associate, Institute of Defence Studies and Analyses, New Delhi.

Anne Marchal is First Counsellor and Head of Section, Political Affairs, Delegation of the European Union to India, New Delhi.

S.D. Muni is currently Distinguished Fellow at the IDSA. He was India's Special Envoy to Southeast Asian countries on UN Security Council Reforms (2005-2006) and served as India's Ambassador to Lao PDR (1997-1999). He superannuated from Jawaharlal Nehru University, New Delhi in 2006 and had held the Appadorai Chair of International Relations and Area Studies. He was the founder Editor of *Indian Foreign Affairs Journal* (Cambridge University Press, India) and *South Asia Journal* (Sage India). He served the Observer Research Foundation, New Delhi, as Director of Research (2006-2007). Prof. Muni was nominated to India's first National Security Advisory Board in 1990-91. His recent publications include *The Emerging Dimension of SAARC* (2010), *India's Foreign Policy: The Democracy Factor* (2009), *India and China: The Next Decade* (2009) and *China's Strategic Engagement with the New ASEAN* (2002).

Gulshan Sachdeva is Chairperson and Professor, Centre for European Studies, School of International Studies, Jawaharlal Nehru University, New Delhi. He has been Visiting Professor, University of Antwerp (2008), University of Trento (2008-2009), Corvinus University, Budapest (2011) and Mykolas Romers University, Vilnius, Lithuania (October 2013). He has also been a consultant with the Institute of Conflict Management, New Delhi.

Manish Thapa is Assistant Professor, Department of Peace and Conflict Studies, Tribhuvan University, Kathmandu. He holds a Ph.D. in International Studies from the Department of International Studies, The University of Tokyo. He has held a number of fellowships, including Erasmus Mundus Visiting Scholar, Institute for International Relations and Center for Contemporary India Research and Studies, University of Warsaw and Robert McNamara Visiting Research Fellow, Department of Peace and Conflict Research, Uppsala University, Sweden (Jan-Jun 2010). He is the author/editor/co-editor of a number of books including *India in the Contemporary World* (Delhi/London: Routledge, 2014), *Internal Conflicts and Peace-building Challenges* (New Delhi: New Century Publication, 2011) and *Concepts and Ideas in Peace, Conflict and Security Studies* (Kathmandu: Mandala Books, 2009).

Preface

Conflict resolution has been a major concern of the European Union. During the European Political Cooperation (1970-1993), conflict resolution was not an explicit policy goal. However, it remained the overriding concern in almost all particular contexts that European diplomacy engaged. Conflict prevention has become "a central idea and a prime hope" of the Common Foreign and Security Policy (CFSP) set up by the Maastricht Treaty (1993) so much so that the EU has felt that its own attempts at conflict prevention may "apply globally, if not comprehensively". (European Commission, "Communication from the Commission on Conflict Prevention," COM (2001) 211 Final, 11 April 2001). A decade later, the European Security Strategy (2003) urged the Union to engage in a full range of conflict resolution activities including conflict prevention, crisis management and post-violence rehabilitation. With the ratification of the Lisbon Treaty (2009), the Union's external action would aim towards "preserving peace, preventing conflicts and strengthening security" (Article III-193 (2c)). The Treaty also identified a clear link between the "EU's internal nature and its external projection" after "having secured peace internally, the Union's foreign policy vocation would be to promote peace externally, drawing on and promoting the principles on which it is founded" that include democracy, human rights, fundamental freedoms and the rule of law along with inter-state cooperation and integration (Article I-2 and I-3 of the Lisbon Treaty). Thus, the link between principles such as human rights, democracy, rule of law, and regional cooperation on the one hand and the prevention and resolution of conflicts on the other are inherent in the EU's approach to conflict resolution.

Since the late 1990s, the EU's conflict resolution activities have encompassed short-, medium- as well as long-term efforts ranging from civilian and military crisis management, conflict settlement to state-building, democratization and societal reconciliation. The goal of such measures was to foster sustainable structural change in third countries, which, in turn, was expected to facilitate conflict prevention, resolution and transformation. Beyond its own borders, the Union has felt that it can contribute to conflict prevention by promoting political liberalization, by making economic assistance conditional upon democratic reform, fostering development of civil society and non-governmental organizations, and insistence on the protection of human rights. However, the contribution of the European Union to conflict resolution beyond its own borders has been marginal.

This book contains eight chapters, which are revised versions of papers which were presented at the international conference on "India, Europe and Conflict Resolution in South Asia" organized at the School of International Studies, Jawaharlal Nehru University on 1-2 March 2012. The first chapter critically evaluates the types of conflict in South Asia and discusses their causes and consequences as well as the challenges and prospects of conflict in the region. The second and third chapters examine the capabilities, priorities, role and importance of conflict resolution in EU foreign policy. The remaining chapters of the volume focus on the European Union's role in conflict resolution in Afghanistan, Nepal, Sri Lanka, and Myanmar. The volume also evaluates the role of Norway in conflict resolution in Sri Lanka and assesses its performance as a facilitator, as a member of the Sri Lanka Monitoring Mission (SLMM), and as an aid donor.

The seminar on "India, Europe and Conflict Resolution in South Asia" and publication of this volume was made possible under Grant No. 2010-3113 for the JNU Jean Monnet Chair from the Lifelong Learning Programme of the European Commission. This volume reflects the views only of the contributors, and the Commission cannot be held responsible for any use which may be made of the information contained therein.

Rajendra K. Jain

1
Conflicts in South Asia: Causes, Consequences, Prospects

S.D. Muni

Studying conflicts is a big intellectual enterprise. More than sixty per cent of the top 100 think tanks listed in a University of Pennsylvania survey in 2012 study conflicts and related issues. These conflict studies concentrate mostly on inter-state wars and intra-state armed conflicts.[1] The conflicts generated by great power interventions or the imperatives of global order inducing and intensifying conflicts receive only occasional or incidental attention. This area of conflict studies would perhaps gain in salience as the global strategic order becomes more turbulent to redefine itself, the phenomenon of "Arab Spring" spreads even to other regions, and interventions invoking the "Responsibility to Protect (R2P)" within the framework of the United Nations are more frequently invoked as in Libya, or possibly Syria. Moreover, the role of "global political conditions" needs to be factored in seriously in the study of conflicts. Making this point, Spain's former Foreign Minister and the former Secretary-General of North Atlantic Treaty Organization (NATO) Javier Solana and the President of Eurasia Group Ian Bremmer jointly commented (21 January 2013):

> In today's world, identifying and managing hotspots is not simply a matter of pulling out a map, spotting the wildfires and empowering diplomats to douse the flames. To understand today's major conflicts and confrontations, we must recognize important ways in which global political conditions enable them. Conflicts

> are much more likely to arise or persist when those with the means to prevent or end them cannot and will not do so.[2]

One may even go further than this and say that conflicts will persist until the major powers of the world and the global power system that they create continue to perpetuate, manage, and exacerbate them (conflicts) for their (great powers') strategic and other interests. In conflict studies, the questions of resource conflicts and human security concerns have been neglected until the end of the last millennium. It is only recently that they are being increasingly taken up but with inadequate efforts and resources.

South Asia has earned a status of its own as an important area of focus in conflict studies, and why not? After all, it is a region which has witnessed five full-scale interstate conflicts, where adversaries are major Asian powers armed with nuclear weapons. Some South Asian states have earned the distinction of becoming part of the global terrorism hub and where no country has been free from insurgencies and separatist movements. A large number of South Asian think tanks, including those funded by governments and affiliated to established universities, are involved in conflict studies. One of them based in New Delhi, the Institute of Peace and Conflict Studies (IPCS), has been running an annual conference on the study of "Armed Conflicts in South Asia" for the past seven years.[3] In this chapter, we propose to identify the types of conflict in South Asia and discuss their causes and consequences.

Types of Conflict

Conflicts in South Asia as in most other parts of the world can be broadly put in four categories, viz. (i) those generated, perpetuated and fuelled by the global political, strategic and developmental dynamics including the role of great powers; (ii) those resulting from direct state-to-state conflicts; (iii) those precipitated by the internal political turbulence and protests; and (iv) those that are caused and nurtured by the non-state actors. The first category includes conflicts inflicted by the forces and factors from outside the region.

For example, the first category comprises conflict generated in or between the South Asian countries as a result of the US post-9/11 intervention in Afghanistan to wage a "global war on terrorism", the Soviet military intervention in Afghanistan in 1979-80 and the US-led resistance to this intervention during 1980-89—both propelled by the exigencies of the Cold War. The Chinese war on India (1962) was also a war inflicted on a South Asian country from outside the region. The Cold War had also impinged on South Asia to deepen and sharpen regional divides and complicate issues like the Kashmir dispute between India and Pakistan. Besides the strategic aspects of the world order, its developmental and ideological impact has also stimulated and reinforced many internal conflicts. For instance, besides its many positive implications, the process of globalisation has also had a negative fallout, which has added to South Asian woes and worries.[4]

In the second category, India–Pakistan conflicts would assume an important place. There have been other inter-state bilateral tensions and conflicts in South Asia like those between Pakistan and Afghanistan, India and Sri Lanka on Sri Lanka's ethnic question, between Nepal and Bhutan on the issue of Bhutanese refugees, etc. The third category would include all the insurgencies and ethnic/sectarian conflicts in South Asia ranging from Afghanistan's Taliban and Al Qaeda to Pakistan's Baluchistan/Shia–Sunni conflict, India's Kashmir, Northeast and Left extremist insurgencies, Nepal's Maoist insurgency, and Sri Lanka's ethnic conflict. The last category would comprise the activities of various cross-border terrorist groups, including the attacks on Mumbai in India (2008) or the operations of the insurgent and criminal groups across the borders in South Asia.

The conflicts included in these categories could both be armed and violent as well as those that manifest diplomatic tensions, strong disagreements and non-violent popular protests. Both armed and unarmed conflicts have a tendency to feed into each other and get transformed into each other. The science and art of conflict management generally focuses on transforming violent conflicts into non-violent ones and preventing the non-violent conflicts from assuming violent dimensions. Non-violent inter-state conflicts in South Asia have been triggered by territorial disputes, disagreements on access to or sharing of resources of the region like water or energy, breakdown of or difficulties in the flow of trade and investments, migration of people across the borders, etc.

The fourth category of conflicts, related to the operations of non-state actors, is receiving greater attention in recent years, especially after the 9/11 Al Qaeda attacks on the United States and the proliferation of terrorist groups that operate with or without the support of any established state. Underlining the importance of non-state actors in conflict studies, India's former National Security Adviser Shivshankar Menon in his address to the Institute of Peace and Conflict Studies (IPCS) Conference in 2012 stated:

> Today, there is a fundamental change in the nature of conflict, which is not just evolving from one stage to another, but is undergoing change as a result of shift in the character of a conflict. The age of global interdependence has ensured the decline in conflicts between states. Nevertheless, there is escalation in the conflicts involving non-state actors, particularly when the lines between state and non-state actors are considerably becoming vague. . . .The cocktail of NGOs, social media and the like, as spotted in West Asia, induce kinetic and physical consequences ultimately culminating in regime changes. In addition, the technology has also empowered the non-state actors to pose an important challenge to the state. The obliteration of distinction between state and non-state actors along with the punctured boundaries of state sovereignty has created new situations demanding novel perspectives.[5]

The above-mentioned categories of conflicts are analytical categories and the conflicts thus generated do not necessarily remain confined to any single category. Quite often it is the spillover of one into another category of conflict that make the real-life conflicts complex and intricate for both states and analysts to address. In this context, one can recall the 1971 Indo-Pakistan war that led to the emergence of a sovereign independent Bangladesh. This inter-state conflict was generated by the internal turbulence within Pakistan, by the military regime's authoritarian and ruthless way of dealing with the demands of the Bengalis of then East Pakistan. This has been admitted even in the Pakistan government appointed Humdoor Rahman Commission Report. This is not to deny India's strategic interests in exploiting Pakistan's internal turbulence, but such interests could not have come into play if there was no internal conflict in Pakistan and the spillover of this conflict did not affect India adversely. The spillover of this conflict and the indifference of the international community towards these consequences forced India to get involved. Strategic interests in the context of the then prevailing Cold War and the American military alliance with Pakistan sucked the United States and China into the regional inter-state conflict.[6]

The above-mentioned categories of conflicts in South Asia also do not represent any chronological or hierarchical order. There is a general assumption globally, and for good reasons, that inter-state conflicts have increasingly given way to the conflicts within states.[7] South Asia is no exception to this but the boundaries of conflicts should be seen as porous and not rigid in South Asia and elsewhere. Moreover, the trends in conflict types are also not unilinear. Howsoever remote it looks, the possibility of another India–Pakistan war or even an open India–China conflict or India facing a two-front war situation exists in reality.[8] Some of the most intractable and protracted internal conflicts in South Asia like the ethnic conflict in Sri Lanka and the Maoist insurgency in Nepal have been brought to an end in rather unexpected ways. No one predicted either a total military annihilation of the Liberation Tigers of Tamil Eelam (LTTE) in Sri Lanka at the hands of the Sri Lankan military in 2009 or the acceptance of a peaceful, democratic transformation by the Nepalese Maoists through quiet and informal Indian good offices in 2006.[9] However, bringing an end to a conflict does not necessarily signify that it has been resolved, and that its root causes have been fully addressed and eliminated. In Sri Lanka, even after the end of the war, the political resolution of the ethnic issue is awaited and the promise of building a New Nepal, that brought the Maoists into the mainstream of national politics, remains to be fulfilled and institutionalised though the Monarchy has been removed and a republican political order has been established.

The Causes

Two major roots of South Asian conflicts have been their colonial legacies and turbulent processes of post-independence nation- and state-building. Three sets of colonial legacies, which had considerable conflict potential, were (i) the creation of unnatural and absurd state systems, (ii) the unresolved boundaries of these states, and (iii) undefined status of a diversity of its ethnic and religious minorities and social groups. The end of colonial rule in South Asia was the result, not of any war of independence, but a peaceful struggle waged by India.

The success of this struggle ensured the decolonisation of other South Asian countries like Myanmar (then Burma) and Sri Lanka (then Ceylon) as well. However, the partition of India created an unnatural and absurd state of Pakistan as a two-piece entity, in the east and the west, separated by a huge chunk of Indian territory. This absurdity was rationalised only 23 years after partition and as a result of a fierce regional conflict, when Bangladesh emerged as a separate sovereign, independent nation in 1971. The communal rationale of partition, though endorsed for shortsighted political gains by the Indian National Congress and the Muslim League, had a strong strategic undercurrent to create a strong and subservient Muslim state that could rally other oil-rich Muslim states of the region and resist the feared Soviet march southwards. The traditional British colonial interests converged here with the emerging American interests that shaped the contours of the Cold War in strategically dividing the whole world. The communal basis of the state of Pakistan, however, kept Pakistan internally uncertain of its national identity and left a potentially volatile unending cause of communal conflict simmering not only between India and Pakistan but also within both countries.

The absurdity of the transfer of power was also inherent in the application of the principle of paramountcy. This principle not only made the task of building and consolidating new states in India and Pakistan difficult and conflict-prone but contributed to the persisting source of tensions and war between them, such as on the Kashmir question.[10] A colonial mindset to keep India and Pakistan divided was evident in many other forms as well. Recall India's first British Governor General Mountbatten's insistence on India's independent government for 'accession' and 'plebiscite' on the Kashmir issue at the same time. Accession as a condition to India's defence of Kashmir against Pakistan's tribal invasion prevented Pakistan from seizing Kashmir by military means and the 'plebiscite' rider on accession prevented India to fully integrate Kashmir with the Indian Union.

The colonial legacy of an unresolved border also continues to keep relations among South Asian nations conflict prone. Two of the longest imperial boundaries of the British India left unsettled were with Afghanistan (Durand Line) and China (McMahon Line). While the former is a major contentious issue between Afghanistan and Pakistan, the latter resulted in a war between India and China in 1962 and continues to be vulnerable to another Sino-Indian conflict. Tensions have also cropped up between China and Bhutan due to the unsettled McMahon Line between British India and Tibet. The Radcliffe partition line between India and (East) Pakistan has not yet become a settled boundary between India and Bangladesh. The two countries signed a boundary agreement in 1974 and again in September 2011, which resolved the complicated question of enclaves of one country into the territory of another. However, both these agreements have yet to be ratified by the Indian parliament owing to internal political pressures. The unfinished business of firming up the Radcliffe Line also keeps the India–Pakistan border fragile and sensitive in the Sir Creek area. It is also unfortunate that India and Pakistan left the task of drawing the Line of Control (LOC) incomplete after the Simla Agreement of 1972, resulting in the bilateral conflict in the Siachen Glacier region. Disputes on defining borders have also haunted India in its relations with both

Sri Lanka and Nepal. The India–Sri Lanka border has been settled peacefully following the agreement on Kachchativu Island (1974) and the settlement of the maritime boundary in the Palk Strait (1976). In the case of Nepal, the boundary issue gets complicated by the changing course of common rivers with India.

Many South Asian conflicts, as stated earlier, result from the sources located outside the region, in the global political and strategic order. A more than a decade-long "war on global terrorism" that has engulfed two major South Asian countries, viz. Afghanistan and Pakistan, directly and India indirectly, resulted from the US attack and intervention in Afghanistan in 2001. The American attack on Al Qaeda in Afghanistan can in many legitimate ways be explained as an act of retaliation against Al Qaeda's 9/11 aggression and the acts of unprecedented terrorism on the United States. However, there was something more in the 9/11 attacks than just an act of terrorism. To say that terrorism was a collateral damage may amount to stretching the argument a bit too far, but one must objectively assess that the three attacks on the White House, the Pentagon and the World Trade Centre were carefully chosen targets of the American political, military and economic power. The targets were not the American people but the icons of American power and dominance which the Al Qaeda has been resenting and preparing to challenge. 9/11 in another way was therefore an attack on the unipolar global political order as it existed after the end of the Cold War. American and NATO forces were scheduled to withdraw from Afghanistan by July 2014. However, the nature of the end game in Afghanistan and its consequences for conflict in South Asia remain to be seen.

This is however not for the first time that an extra-regional power's intervention or an imperative of the global political dynamics has resulted in conflict in South Asia. The Soviet intervention in Afghanistan in December 1979 was an even worse example of an extra-regional intervention in South Asia which also involved Pakistan in the ensuing conflict. The strong impulse of Cold War between the then prevailing superpowers was clearly the driving force behind this intervention. While the Soviet Union explained its intervention as a reaction to American covert operations in Afghanistan, considered to be the soft under-belly of its Central Asian region, the United States regarded the Soviet military push as an attempt to access the warm waters of the Indian Ocean through Pakistan. Washington, therefore, exerted all its efforts, in collaboration with the countries like Pakistan, to roll it back. China had joined the US as the Cold War had taken on a new dimension, leading to China's split from its ideological alliance with the Soviet Union and brought it closer to the US to help settle its differences with the former communist ally.

Yet another example of a war inflicted on a South Asian country from outside the region was the Sino-Indian conflict of 1962. This war has generally been presented in history textbooks as a border war precipitated by a territorial dispute between Asian's giant neighbours. So it was in many respects. However, if China initiated this war only in pursuance of its territorial claims to settle the issue with India then why did it withdraw almost completely and unilaterally even from the areas that it continues to lay its claims on, like Tawang, Arunachal Pradesh and parts of Sikkim? Beijing, of course, continues to keep the disputed Aksai Chin region in the western sector of the Himalayan border under its occupation since 1958, much before the war of 1962. The decision to launch the attack on India was surreptitiously taken by Chairman Mao Zedong, in consultation with a coterie of close advisers around him and not through the legitimate organs of the Chinese State. What irritated Chairman Mao and the Chinese leadership most, more than India's refusal to accept the Chinese proposal of a package deal by swapping the territories claimed, was the feeling of China's isolation. India was seen to be enjoying support both from the United States and the Soviet Union. If this support continued, India could emerge as the major Asian power which was unacceptable to China. The war of 1962 therefore humiliated India militarily in Asia and exposed the extent of poor support that the two superpowers could extend to India in its hour of need. China chose the right time to launch its attack when both the superpowers were trapped in the worst moment of their mutual rivalry, viz the nuclear standoff in Cuba.

There are also reports that China had diplomatically ascertained that the US was not in a position to come to India's help if the latter got involved in any conflict.

The above instances underline the role of the then prevailing global strategic system, with the Cold War playing an important role in imposing conflicts on South Asian countries. The Cold War had also widened and sharpened the India–Pakistan divide and made the Kashmir conflict intractable. Cultivating Pakistan as a bulwark of Muslim anti-communist resistance against the Soviet Union in the energy-rich Central and West Asian regions was an important objective of the US-led Western alliance system. In return, Pakistan demanded support on the Kashmir question; a relatively small price that the United States was more than willing to pay. The American military establishments were also hopeful that Pakistan would be willing to spare troops for necessary Asian operations of the Western alliance system if the Kashmir issue could be settled to its satisfaction. Prime Minister Jawaharlal Nehru tried in vain to resolve the Kashmir issue in cooperation with Pakistan before the latter could be inducted into the Western alliance system.[11] During the early years of the Cold War, the US drive to contain China also resulted in complicating the Tibetan question as a result of the Dalai Lama's flight to India and the waging of a covert anti-China war in Tibet through the Tibetan tribe of the Khampas. These developments contributed to the breakdown of the "*Hindi-Chini Bhai Bhai*" phase in Sino-Indian relations and deterioration in these relations on the border and Tibetan issues. While these issues remain unresolved, the transformation of great power relations from the Cold War to the emerging rivalry between China and the United States provides China with the potential to foster greater conflict between China and India.

The strategic dimensions of the world order have directly interfered with the conflicts in South Asia. However, its ideological and developmental aspects have created conditions that have encouraged, intensified and sustained conflicts in South Asian societies. Globalisation has not only opened up greater opportunities for South Asian countries, but has also induced distortions by widening inequalities, creating and sustaining poverty, enhancing consumerism, encouraging crony capitalism and intensifying cultural alienation. These distortions in the developmental processes have generated conditions for conflicts identified in the World Bank Conflict Analysis Framework.[12] Globalisation has unleashed three explosions in the developing countries like those in South Asia, viz. of information, identity and aspirations. Political systems have not been able to cope with the imperatives of these explosions, in the face of severe governance and leadership deficits. A telling example of the governance deficit is evident in the failure of the South Asian regimes not only in leaving large social constituencies and marginalised sections ungoverned and un/under-developed but also in not rehabilitating large numbers of people uprooted as a result of mega developmental projects like high dams, mining and deforestation.[13] Numerous examples of leadership failure in South Asia in recent years are evident in the failure of institutionalising democratic gains in Nepal, Maldives and Pakistan, and thus creation of potential for conflicts. Even after four years of defeating the Tamil insurgency, the ruling regime in Sri Lanka has failed to find credible answers to the root causes of the ethnic conflict. Excessive preoccupation with personal and group (party) power has been the single-most reason behind the leadership failures in such cases. Struggles for power and influence at various levels in the South Asian polities have sustained and vitiated raging conflicts. Some of these typical examples include the political use of Sikh extremist Bhindranwale in Punjab during the 1970s by India's Indira Gandhi, hobnobbing of the Sri Lankan President Ranasinghe Premadasa with the Liberation Tigers of Tamil Eelam (LTTE) to humiliate the Indian Peace Keeping Force (IPKF) during the late 1980s and the patronising of the Maoist insurgency by King Birendra of Nepal during 1996-2001. Excessive, unplanned and indiscriminate use of force by South Asian states in dealing with internal revolts and insurgencies have accelerated these conflicts and made them even more intractable.

South Asian domestic conflicts are also rooted in its turbulent and unfinished processes of state- and nation-building. Unsettled social equations and political hierarchies sharpen ethnic and sectarian conflicts. Identity and ownership of the state and the nation in the making bring diverse social groups at daggers drawn. For instance, Pakistan's unsettled national identity with the dominance of Punjabis over Sindhi, Baluchi and Pathan social groups, and Sri Lanka's decision in 1959 to carve itself out as a Sinhala-Buddhist State ignoring the sensitivities of the Tamil and Muslim minority have been at the root of serious internal conflicts in these countries. In over 65 years of democratic evolution, India too had to confront numerous challenges of integrating marginalised social groups. The upsurge of hitherto neglected and discriminated caste and tribal groups are putting huge pressure on the capacities of the state and its political processes. The unequal distribution of the fruits of development and a widening gap between aspirations and acquisitions of social groups also fuel conflicts. In Nepal, the ten years of Maoist insurgency from 1996 to 2006 were sustained by the marginalised tribal and regional groups who are now demanding an equal and respectable status in 'New Nepal'. This, in turn, has contributed towards the difficulties in the process of both Constitution writing and institution building.

South Asia's unnatural and open borders along with its contiguous ethnic and social spread has easily allowed one country's internal conflicts to spillover into the other, leading to bilateral conflicts. Such spillover(s) have been spurred by conscious decisions of one country to employ and exploit the internal conflicts of its neighbouring country in pursuance of its strategic, foreign or domestic policy interests. Most South Asian countries are guilty of exploiting their neighbour's predicament in this respect at one time or another. India's involvement in Sri Lanka's ethnic conflict and the emergence of Bangladesh, Pakistan's cross-border terrorism against India and Afghanistan, Nepal's resentment over the flow of Nepali refugees from Bhutan are well known examples of internal conflicts becoming bilateral and regional conflicts in South Asia. Some of these transformed conflicts have also been resolved by a radical shift in the policies of the aggravating state towards the conflict-affected state and by forging greater cooperation to deal with its spillover effects. India's shift from helping the Tamil insurgency to fighting the LTTE in 1987 through the IPKF may be seen as a representative example of such radical policy shifts.[14] There are signs of such a shift since 2010 in Bangladesh's attitude towards India's northeast insurgent groups seeking support and shelter in its territory.[15] It may not be out of place to mention here that India succeeded in enlisting credible cooperation from Bhutan (in 2003) and Myanmar (1995) in launching joint operations against insurgent groups operating in India but seeking shelter and sanctuaries in these countries.

The Consequences

The consequences of the South Asian conflicts are clearly evident on the structure of its states as well as on the societies that constitute these states. We noted earlier that conflicts were inherent in the way South Asian states were structured after the colonial rule, and these inherent conflicts, in turn, also restructured them. Three examples stand out in this respect. An obvious example is the question of Kashmir which has at least temporarily altered the boundaries of India and Pakistan. It is not possible to say at this stage as to what the eventual solution of the Kashmir problem would be. But it needs to be kept in mind that a large chunk (nearly 5,000 sq. kms.) of its occupied Kashmir in the Himalayas was ceded by Pakistan to China under its boundary agreement concluded in 1963. Though the agreement left room for renegotiating this boundary after the final resolution of Kashmir between India and Pakistan, but one wonders if China would ever transfer the ceded territory if and when the whole of Kashmir (including the Pakistan occupied) *de facto* becomes a part of India. Another example is that of the creation of Bangladesh in 1971 out of the absurdly structured Pakistan, as a result of a fierce conflict between India and Pakistan which involved the United States, China and the United Nations. The third example was that of Sikkim, a British protectorate in the Himalayas, inherited by India as a protectorate ruled by its feudal king, the Chogyal. As a result of internal conflict between Sikkim's majority Nepali community led by Lhendup Dorji and the Chogyal, Sikkim abandoned its feudal ruler, ended its protectorate status and became an integral part of the Indian Union in April 1975.[16]

The question of redefining and restructuring South Asia's state structure as a result of its conflicts remains relevant. The military elimination of the LTTE has closed the option of a separate Tamil Eelam, but if the ethnic question is not resolved politically and amicably, the re-emergence of separatist Tamil tendencies in future cannot be ruled out. In India, the persisting conflicts in the Northeast especially of the Nagas and Kashmir, have the viruses of separatism, though one hopes that India's resilient polity and gradually strengthening State would not let these issues explode. In Nepal, if the Terai region is not integrated through a federal structure and socio-economic accommodation, many Nepalese are apprehensive that the separatist demand would gain momentum. There is however, no support for Terai separatism in India.[17] Pakistan is also afflicted by the separatist sentiments in Baluchistan which is facing an insurgency. Pakistan's frontier province facing Afghanistan continues to have strong separatist sentiments based on Pashtun identity. There is a serious debate among analysts and policy-makers if Pakistan would be able to keep its unity and territorial integrity intact in the face of multiple internal conflicts and religious extremism.[18] Many analysts are concerned that the uncertainty in Afghanistan particularly after the US and NATO withdrawal may result in a violent redefining of the Afghan state and Pakistan–Afghanistan border.[19]

In addition to creating new states and altering state boundaries, conflicts in South Asia have also changed regimes and political systems. Some of the representative examples may be flagged here. The 1971 India–Pakistan conflict that resulted in a humiliating defeat for the Pakistan army enabled the first popularly elected civilian regime headed by Zulfikar Ali Bhutto to last for a full-term of five years since the birth of Pakistan. The army again staged a comeback in 1977 after the elections, but that could become possible due to the weakening of the civilian regime and resurgence of the army due to the conflict in Baluchistan. The Maoists insurgency in Nepal encouraged King Gyanendra in 2002 to thwart democratic governance and take power directly into his hands in 2005. However, the success of the *Jan Andolan* II (Peoples' Uprising II) in April 2006, which resulted from the Maoists joining hands with the mainstream political parties, led finally (in 2008) to the abolition of Monarchy and establishment of a republican democratic order. In Sri Lanka, ethnic conflict was a driving force behind the 1982 Constitution that established the presidential system. Fresh debates have been revived in Sri Lanka if this is indeed the best system. Even when systems and regimes have not been changed substantially, conflicts have induced incremental changes in the institutions of governance, especially those dealing with law and order, the judiciary and the development of social sectors. The strengthening of the institutions of national security, including military, police and intelligence agencies has been a common feature in most South Asian countries. Some states like Pakistan, and to a certain extent Sri Lanka, display characteristics of being national security states.

Conflicts have also brought in violence to South Asian societies in a big way. Many of the prominent South Asian leaders like Indira Gandhi and Rajiv Gandhi of India, President Premadasa and prominent ministers Lalith Athulathmudali, Gamini Dissanayake, Ranjan Wijeratne and Lakshman Kadirgamar (and many others) of Sri Lanka, and Benazir Bhutto of Pakistan were killed in the wake of conflicts. The death of innocent South Asians in civil wars and terrorist attacks run into thousands and with women and children subjected to untold abuses.[20] Such widespread violence and transmission of gory images through television into the South Asian living rooms are adding to the brutalisation of societies. South Asian conflicts have also made this region a prominent place for the recruitment of child soldiers. South Asian conflicts have significantly contributed to the deepening and aggravation of ethnic, communal and sectarian fault-lines and identity-based polarisation which has further fuelled political fragmentation and instability.

The impact of conflicts on economic growth and social development may be a matter of debate in South Asia. Many experts argue that there are examples of conflict areas being quarantined to let economic activity go uninterrupted. For instance, the dynamism of Sri Lanka's tourism and garment manufacturing sectors remaining unaffected by its ethnic conflict is often being referred to in this respect. Similarly, the Indian economy has witnessed impressive growth while continuing to cope with internal and external conflicts. However, these examples are not very definitive as contrary examples of the countries like Nepal, Pakistan and Afghanistan recording poor growth under the impact of conflicts also exist simultaneously. There is however no denying the fact that conflicts escalate opportunity costs in the affected countries. In India, it has been publicly admitted at the highest political levels that the Left extremist insurgency is a major deterrent to India's growth. With the ending of insurgencies in Nepal and Sri Lanka, prospects of growth have brightened. Leaders of India, Pakistan and China have also repeatedly stressed that peaceful relations between them are necessary to maintain the momentum of growth and development. It is acknowledged in South Asia that one of the greatest obstacles to the success of regional cooperation under the South Asian Association for Regional Cooperation (SAARC) has been the conflict between India and Pakistan. As bilateral trade channels are being activated between the two countries, it is hoped that regional trade will grow to the advantage of all the member countries. Conflict and regional rivalry between India and Pakistan is also obstructing the prospects of their mutual cooperation with Afghanistan, which, if facilitated, can in turn help both Pakistan and Afghanistan fight their internal insurgencies better.[21]

Conflicts in South Asia have impinged adversely on the autonomy of the region and its countries. They have made the South Asian states porous and vulnerable to external interventions and influences. Such influences have been both benign and destructive. It has been well documented that the

India–Pakistan conflict facilitated the induction of the global Cold War in the region and this induction further deepened the regional conflict.[22] Pakistan which was initially enthusiastic of the American alliance subsequently resented it.[23] In the context of the US role in the "war on terror" in Afghanistan, the US presence and influence in Pakistan has become a major issue of national controversy, particularly after the American intelligence operation to kill Osama bin Laden in his Pakistani hideout. Sri Lanka's invitation to Norway for facilitating talks with the LTTE in the year 2000 eventually was criticised and stopped by the Rajapaksa regime. At the regional level, India's involvement in Sri Lanka during the 1980s and in Nepal during 2005-2006 in resolving their respective insurgencies also eventually came under heavy criticism.

Thus, we find that consequences of conflicts on South Asia have been diverse and damaging. These consequences have affected all the vital sectors of life in the region such as security, stability, political order, economic development and social dynamics. The South Asian people need to learn from these conflicts and commit themselves to resolving them in the interests of their own security and well being.

Prospects

Conflicts are inherent in human nature and they are an integral part of states and societies.[24] South Asia or any other region cannot be an exception in this respect. Almost all the causes of South Asian conflicts listed in this chapter ranging from historical legacies to turbulent state and nation-building processes and the distorted developmental dynamics continue to be relevant. Even when one set of conflicts is resolved, another set appears and gets entrenched, maybe in a somewhat transformed or redefined form.

The root causes of conflict between Pakistan and India as well as China and India remain unmitigated despite efforts to put in place confidence-building measures (CBMs). Between India and Pakistan, the Kashmir question remains unresolved and the spillover of Pakistan's internal identity crisis and dominance of the army in politics that generate instruments of conflict like cross-border terrorism continue to thrive, undercutting the expression of peaceful intent and CBMs. Any repeat of a Mumbai-type cross-border terror attack or violation of the Line of Control (LOC) ceasefire like Kargil or otherwise, can trigger passions and political moves leading to an unmanageable situation. The rise of the Taliban in Afghanistan and *jihadi* extremism in Pakistan may create conditions for such an attack. Generally, however, Pakistan is expected to be preoccupied with its north-western front Afghanistan and would want to keep the eastern front with India peaceful and stable.

Both India and China have stakes in peace and stability so that their growth dynamics can go uninterrupted. China's deepening engagement on territorial disputes with Japan and South China Sea neighbours hopefully will keep it keen on having peace and understanding with India. China's new leadership has also laid greater emphasis on its perceived core interests in the South China Sea where war drums are sounding louder than ever.[25] Despite the imperative of keeping the India front peaceful and stable, China seems less prepared to resolve the border issue and is worried about the possible firming up of strategic partnership between the United States and India, impinging on its interests in the Asia-Pacific region, particularly the South China Sea. In such a situation, China making moves to disturb India either directly on the pretext of border and the Tibetan issues, or indirectly by encouraging Pakistan to keep India engaged on its western front cannot be ruled out. In 1962, as stated earlier, India's strategic equations with the United States and the then USSR were a major factor prompting China to undertake the border offensive.

Inter-state conflicts within South Asia, barring the India–Pakistan dyad, may be ruled out for any foreseeable future. There could however be tensions on a number of other issues from the spillover of internal conflicts to the sharing of resources (common rivers, territorial waters and extended maritime economic zone, trade and investment-related issues, human migration etc.), but outright war looks improbable and unrealistic. However, internal conflicts within South Asian countries are not likely to be coming to an end in the foreseeable future. India's insurgencies (Kashmir, the Northeast and Left extremism) will persist. The Indian state is resilient in dealing with identity challenges and has also shown promise in coping with ideological insurgency. However, the task of coordinating state actions in a divisive and federal polity with highly bureaucratised state institutions is not an easy one. This will pose a major challenge to the new and enthusiastic government of Narendra Modi who wants to give new dynamism to India both economically and politically. Tensions within Sri Lanka on the ethnic question do not seem to be dying out. In Bangladesh, Pakistan and Afghanistan, Islamic extremism and sectarian clashes may experience a surge and in Nepal the breakaway faction of the Maoists continue to adhere to the concept of "peoples' war".

The capabilities of the South Asian states to effectively respond to, manage and/or resolve these internal conflicts would depend critically on two aspects, viz. the institutionalisation of democratic functioning and the guarantee of a respectable rate of economic growth with distributive justice. Both of these have so far proved to be formidable challenges in most of the South Asian countries. For example, both Nepal and Maldives have so far failed to institutionalise the democratic achievements gained in the first decade of the twenty-first century. It is to the credit of Pakistan's elected civilian regime led by the Pakistan Peoples' Party that it has completed its full term (only the second time in the entire history of Pakistan so far) but the tensions among the principal governing institutions like the executive, the army and the judiciary look considerably chaotic. These tensions have now been passed on to the Pakistan Muslim League-led government of Nawaz Sharif. The reinforcing of democratic norms and economic growth will also strengthen the South Asian countries from within and will also improve the prospects of regional integration and cooperation among them through SAARC.

Notes

1. Uppsala University in Sweden has been compiling and putting out data on internal and inter-state conflicts on an annual basis since 1988, under the report *State in Armed Conflict.*
2. Javier Solana and Ian Bremmer, "A New Year of Global Conflict," Project IIIV Syndicate, http://www.project.syndicate.org/print/a.new.year.of.global.conflict.by.javier. (accessed on 28 January 2013)
3. See the IPCS report of the "Armed Conflicts in South Asia 2012" for the Sixth Annual Conference. The Conference was addressed by India's National Security Adviser, Shivshankar Menon.
4. For a discussion of the negative aspects of globalisation, including on South Asia, see George Heine and Ramesh Thakur, eds., *The Dark Side of Globalization* (Tokyo: United Nations University Press, 2011).
5. Ibid., p. 4.
6. Considerable literature is available on this conflict. For some representative studies see Mohammad Ayoob and K. Subrahmanyam, *The Liberation War* (New Delhi: S. Chand & Co., 1972); Richard Sisson and Leo E. Rose, *War and Secession: Pakistan, India and the Creation of Bangladesh* (Berkeley: University of California Press, 1990); General Kamal Matinuddin, *Tragedy of Errors: East Pakistan Crisis, 1968-1971* (Lahore: Wajidalis, 1994).
7. International Institute for Democracy and Electoral Assistance, *Democracy, Conflict and Human Security: Pursuing Peace in 21st Century* (Stockholm: IDEA, 2006). Also see the Uppsala University annual reports on *States in Armed Conflicts.*
8. India's Army Chief Gen. Deepak Kapoor told a closed-door army seminar in December 2009 that India was revising its war strategy to prepare for a two-front war with Pakistan and China. *Times of India*, 31 December 2009; also see Nirupama Subramanian, "General Kapoor's remarks betray hostile intent, says Pakistan," *The Hindu*, 3 January 2010.
9. For some idea of India's role in ending Maoist insurgency in Nepal, see, S.D. Muni, "Bringing the Maoists down from the Hills," in Sebastian von Einsiedel, David Malone and Suman Pradhan, eds., *Nepal in Transition: from People's War to Fragile Peace* (New York: Cambridge University Press, 2012), pp. 313-331.
10. The details of British withdrawal and India's partition have been studied from different perspectives. For a somewhat dispassionate account see, Stanley Wolpert, *Shameful Flight: The Last Years of the British Empire in India* (Oxford: Oxford University Press, 2006).
11. See, S.D. Muni, Chapter 3, "South Asia," in Mohammad Ayoob, ed., *Conflict and Intervention in the Third World* (London: Croom Helm, 1980), pp. 38-72. *Man and Development* articles.
12. http://siteresources.worldbank.org/INTCPR/214574-1112883508044/20657757/CAFApril2005.pdf> (accessed on 31 January 2013)
13. Displacement of marginalised populations and alienation of cultural (tribal) groups is considered one of the important reasons behind the rise of Left extremist insurgency in India.
14. S.D. Muni, *Pangs of Proximity* (New Delhi: Sage, 1993).
15. See on this issue: Wasbir Hussain, "Insurgency in India's Northeast: Cross-

border Links and Strategic Alliances," *Frontline*, vol. 17, February 2006, pp. 105-125; S. Binod Kumar Singh, "India–Bangladesh Relations: Continuous Consolidation," *South Asia Terrorism Portal*, 5 February 2013.

16. For a critical assessment of India's role in the integration of Sikkim, see Sunanda K. Datta-Ray, *Smash and Grab: Annexation of Sikkim* (New Delhi: Vikas Publishing House, 1984).
17. See, Nishchal N. Pandey, "Nepal: Terai-Based militancy and its Transnational Implications," *Peace and Security Review*, Vol. 2, no. 2, 2009, pp. 1-18; Bangladesh Institute of Peace and Security Studies, Dhaka. Krishna Hari Puskar, "Seeds of Ethno-Civil War in Terai," http://www.nepalmonitor.com/2007/12/seeds_of-ethno-civil_war_in_nepal_terai.h (accessed on 6 January 2013).
18. See the reports on this theme prepared by important think tanks like the Brookings Institute, Stephen P. Cohen, et al., *The Future of Pakistan*, (Washington, D.C., 2011) and Institute for Defence Studies and Analyses (IDSA), *Pakistan on the Edge* IDSA Pakistan Project Report, 2012), (New Delhi: IDSA).
19. The debate on the break-up of Afghanistan was envisaged by the former US Diplomat Robert D. Blackwill. See his "Plan B in Afghanistan: Why a de Facto Partition is the Least Bad Option" *Foreign Affairs*, January/February 2011. Also see Ramtanu Maitra, "Long-term Planning for A Post-War Afghanistan," *Executive Intelligence Review*, 13 August 2010.
20. A number of human rights watch groups have continuously been drawing attention to these violations of rights to life, dignity and freedom.
21. See Shahid Javed Burki, *South Asia in the New World Order: The Role of Regional Cooperation* (London: Routledge, 2011).
22. See Howard B. Shaffer, *Limits of Influence: America's Role in Kashmir* (Washington, DC: Brookings Institute, 2009); Dennis Kux has written separate books on the US relations with India and Pakistan. Also see Robert McMahon, *Cold War on the Periphery: The United States, India and Pakistan* (New York: Columbia University Press, 1994).
23. See Pakistani President General Mohammad Ayub Khan's autobiography, *Friends Not Masters* (London: Oxford University Press, 1967). Also see Z.A. Bhutto, *The Myth of Independence* (Karachi: Oxford University Press, 1969).
24. For instance, Max Boot's latest study of guerrilla warfare traces its history from 3000BC when guerrillas of different tribes fought against each other. See Max Boot, *Invisible Armies: An Epic History of Guerrilla Warfare from Ancient Times to the Present* (New York: Liveright Publishing Corporation, 2013).
25. Michael Klare, "The Next War", http://www.realclearworld.com/printpage/?url=http;//www.realclearworld.com/articles/. January 23, 2013. (accessed on 29 January 2013).

2
The European Union and Conflict Resolution in South Asia

Anne Marshall

The Importance of Conflict Resolution for the EU

Conflict resolution is in the DNA of the European Union; it is part of our *raison d'être*. The fact that the EU received the Nobel Peace Prize in 2012 came as a surprise to many, and this surprise in itself is proof that the EU has been so successful as a peace-building project that many people now take peace in Europe for granted. This is in stark contrast to Europe's long and bleak history of warfare, with the continent being ravaged by local, national and regional wars in addition to being the origin of the two World Wars. Against this backdrop, the determined efforts to build peace and stability through a gradual process of economic, political and social integration have contributed to a situation today where our interests are so tightly bound to each other that war between EU Member States has become unthinkable if not impossible. As the Norwegian Nobel Committee said when justifying the award of the Peace Prize: "This shows how, through well-aimed efforts and by building up mutual confidence, historical enemies can become close partners."

This historical explanation is important to remember when we talk about some of the conflicts in South Asia today that not so long ago, conflicts between neighbouring countries in Europe also seemed intractable and unsolvable, but there is hope even in the bleakest of cases.

EU Commitments to Conflict Prevention and Resolution

Europe's history of war has profoundly influenced our desire to avoid the same mistakes being made again, whether in Europe or elsewhere in the world. This is what inspires our engagement with neighbouring countries and international partners and ensures that conflict prevention and resolution remain a very current and on-going commitment for the EU. The Lisbon Treaty, which is the foundation of the EU's current role in external affairs, sets as a primary objective for the EU's external action to "preserve peace, prevent conflicts and strengthen international security" (Article 21).

In addition, we have specific documents and commitments that spell out in more detail our commitments to conflict prevention and resolution; in particular, the Gothenburg Programme on Conflict Prevention which was agreed by all EU Member States in 2001. Ten years later, in 2011, the European Council issued conclusions on Conflict Prevention which confirmed that the Gothenburg Programme remains a valid policy basis for further EU action in this field. The Council Conclusions also highlighted areas where progress has been made in implementing the Programme, as well as areas where we need to strengthen our action.

The Role and Added Value of the EU as a Conflict Resolution Actor

In addition to its own history, experience and expertise, the EU today has certain characteristics that make it particularly well placed to support conflict resolution in other parts of the world.

First and foremost, our diversity as a union and our range of available instruments mean that we can employ what we call a comprehensive approach to conflict resolution. We are able to respond to a crisis situation with both short-term and long-term tools and instruments, ranging from political dialogue and security interventions to humanitarian aid and development cooperation, sanctions as well as incentives such as greater access to the EU market.

One current example of where we are trying to employ such a comprehensive approach is the on-going crisis in Mali in West Africa.

Thanks to the military support from France and neighbouring countries in West Africa, the Malian army has been able to liberate most of the north of the country. In support of the same objective, the EU is also providing security-related support through an EU training mission which is helping to restructure and strengthen the capacity of the Malian army and through financial support to the African-led International Support Mission to Mali. To support the victims of the conflict, the EU had increased its humanitarian aid to Mali to €78 million in 2013, in addition to more than €250 million for new development projects across the country. And on the political front, in order to contribute to a lasting solution to the conflict, we are supporting the implementation of the Malian authorities' roadmap to restore democracy and constitutional rule. In addition, we are supporting the electoral process as well as an inclusive national dialogue which, crucially, includes representatives from the troubled North of the country.

Secondly, with 140 EU Delegations around the world, our wide global reach means that we usually have people on the ground who understand the local context and have good local contacts and networks.

Thirdly, as a value-based entity that is above national interests, the EU has a good reputation as a neutral and ethical actor in most parts of the world. This means that the EU is sometimes asked by conflicting parties to be directly involved in negotiations and mediation.

An example of this is the on-going dialogue between Serbia and Kosovo which is facilitated by the EU with the aim to seek normalisation of relations between the two countries. This dialogue has so far led to some concrete positive results including the opening of four border gates, an agreement to appoint liaison officers, and an agreement to protect religious and cultural heritage on both sides of the border.

In some cases of mediation, the EU acts on behalf of the international community. This is the case in the negotiations with Iran, where based on a UN Security Council mandate, and together with the E3+3 (Germany, France, UK + China, Russia, US), the EU is engaging in intense diplomatic efforts to find a negotiated solution to the international community's concerns about the Iranian nuclear programme.

Fourthly, given our history and continuous efforts at deeper and more effective regional cooperation, the EU places great value on international and regional organisations and we have excellent working relationships with most such actors. This leaves us well placed to contribute to joint conflict resolution efforts together with our international and regional partners.

EU Involvement in Conflict Resolution

I have already given some examples of the different ways in which the EU is involved in conflict resolution to explain our added value as an actor in this field. Let me give you a few more examples to show the diversity of our engagement in this field.

The EU is a firm believer in the value of *mediation* as a conflict resolution tool and we therefore have a broad and diverse engagement in different mediation activities. In addition to the so-called Track One negotiations mentioned earlier where the EU is directly involved following requests from the concerned parties, the EU also promotes and supports peace mediation in many other settings. This ranges from preventive diplomacy efforts on the ground by our Heads of Delegation and EU Special Representatives to financial and capacity-building support for local mediation efforts. For example, since last year we are supporting a project through the United Nations which aims to strengthen local capacities for mediation and dialogue in the Maldives. We also recently organised a mediation coaching session for the EU staff in Kabul together with members of the High Peace Council in Afghanistan.

Where a *peace agreement* exists, we often provide direct support to the implementation. One example is in Nepal, where the EU contributes to the consolidation of the peace process by supporting the successful implementation of the Comprehensive Peace Agreement through the Government-run multi-donor Nepal Peace Trust Fund.

We also believe that credible *elections* can be a powerful contributor to stability, and that preventing electoral violence is a critical conflict-prevention activity. The EU is therefore actively supporting preparations for, implementation of and observation of elections in many countries. In South Asia, we are currently providing support to the Independent Election Commissions of Afghanistan and Pakistan. We were one of the major funders of the massive effort to prepare the electoral register and photographic *voter ID* cards ahead of the general elections in Bangladesh in 2008.

In addition to working with Governments, we also work closely with *civil society* actors who play a crucial role in local-level conflict resolution. We actually currently have an open Call for Proposals under which we invite civil society actors to apply for funds for peace-building and conflict prevention projects in South Asia. The deadline for submitting applications was 18 March 2013. Another important issue which is sometimes forgotten in discussions about conflict prevention and conflict resolution is *accountability* and the fight against impunity. In our experience, accountability for past crimes is essential in order to achieve not just the end of war but long-term sustainable peace. We therefore strongly support the strong directives given by the United Nations which exclude the granting of amnesties and immunities for war crimes and crimes against humanities from any UN-sponsored peace agreements. The issue of accountability is currently very topical in the context of Sri Lanka where the EU believes that accountability and justice are critical to ensuring that conflict does not re-erupt. We look forward to the upcoming discussions on this topic in the UN Human Rights Council session in March 2013.

Finally, because I am here to represent the European Union, I have to make the case again for *regional cooperation* as a conflict resolution tool. EU history shows the potential of regional integration and cooperation as a path to peace and prosperity, and we are trying to use our experience to support others who wish to strengthen integration and cooperation in their regions. One of the closest such relationships we have is with the African Union which has come a long way towards regional integration, but we also encourage and support other efforts such as the Heart of Asia initiative in Afghanistan which India is very actively involved in.

Conclusion

To conclude, I hope this brief overview has given you an idea of how the EU's history and set-up makes us well placed to support conflict prevention and conflict resolution. This is of course a big responsibility and while we are doing a lot we can definitely do more, learn lessons from what has worked well or not, and scale up what works well. This is our current and future task. Finally, let me just end with a word of caution. While the EU has its role and added value as a conflict-resolution actor and India has a clear and positive role to play in this field in particular in South Asia, interventions from third parties such as the EU or India is not a magic bullet and we cannot solve other people's conflicts. We can provide support and encouragement, but ultimately peace comes from the efforts of the conflict parties themselves.

3
The European Union and Conflict Resolution

John Doyle

Ireland took over the EU rotating Presidency of the Council of the European Union on 1 January 2013, with the agenda inevitably dominated by the European economic, banking and fiscal crises. Nonetheless, even with a strong economic focus, security and defence policy inevitably played a role in the agenda of the Presidency. The timing was also interesting. Ireland on 31 December 2012 completed its role as Chair in Office of the Organization for Security and Cooperation in Europe (OSCE). That experience for the Ministerial team and the senior officials and military officers involved proved to be very fresh when the EU agenda began.

This chapter explores the priorities in the defence and security arenas during the Irish Presidency and uses that context to discuss the current conflict-resolution capabilities and priorities of the European Union.

European interventions in international security remain a lively topic. France's recent intervention in Mali (January 2013), the French and later the intervention of the North Atlantic Treaty Organization (NATO) in Libya and the continuing European involvement in the NATO mission in Afghanistan all point to a desire by European states to play a role in international security operations on their own and via NATO. However, this is not the comprehensive security strategy combining military capacity, policy, development aid and post-conflict reconstruction promised by the 2003 European Security Strategy (ESS) (December 2003).

Ireland's European Affairs Minister Lucinda Creighton, setting out "Ireland's priorities for the EU Presidency" referred to a broad range of areas, while inevitably focused on economic growth issues. However, while mentioning the growth in EU competences and the post-Lisbon changes, including the European External Action Service, there was no explicit mention of defence or security or conflict resolution (other than energy security and food security).[1] The Irish Government had separately announced an outline defence programme for the Presidency in response to a parliamentary question, with Minister for Defence Alan Shatter TD announcing to Dáil Éireann, that in "consultation with the European External Action Service (EEAS), Ireland will facilitate a formal meeting of the Foreign Affairs Council in Defence Ministers format and a formal defence policy directors' meeting in Brussels". He also declared his

> intention to host, in Ireland, a number of informal meetings and seminars, including a Defence Ministers informal. Usually, the subjects of discussion at the informal meetings range from current military operations, co-operation between the EU and other international organisations, the development of EU military capabilities and on-going developments in the European Defence Agency.[2]

Thus, the Irish Presidency sought to pursue a programme of activity on defence matters, even if its specific agenda was specified and it failed to get mentioned in lists of priority issues.

The EU and Conflict Resolution

The European Union's role as a peace-building organisation is a significant theme in the literature on European integration and in the public discourse of the European Commission and leading European politicians.[3] The discourse of political and Commission elites in particular often conflates the historic experience of the early period of European integration, the claim that war is now "unthinkable" between major European allies with previously conflictual relationships, the European agreed "security complex" and the EU's modern role in external affairs including the development of its foreign, security and defence policies. While there is an extensive critical literature on the limited external engagement of the EU and the difficulties in agreeing to a more comprehensive foreign and security policy, there has been less focus on the weaknesses of the Union in dealing with the limited number of intensive serious conflict within its own borders. The limits of this literature combined with the strength of EU official discourse on the "success" of European integration as a "peace-building project" has led to an exaggerated role for the EU being assumed with consequent over-ambitious hopes being set out for other regional organisations by external observers.

In the case of the South Asian Association for Regional Cooperation (SAARC), it is often reiterated that the strong commitment to state sovereignty is a product of the relatively recent independence of states, compared to most EU Member States and that this combined with the relative weakness of SAARC, even compared to the Association of South East Association Nations (ASEAN) and not only the EU, has made inter-state security rivalries more intense and peace-building more difficult compared to the modern European experience. As the focus of much of the literature is on its potential role in on-going conflicts and inter-state tension within South Asia, this chapter briefly examines the equivalent role of the EU on the Northern Ireland conflict and peace process—the nearest equivalent conflict within the EU—to any of the current conflicts within the borders of SAARC.

Former Irish Foreign Minister Brian Cowen explicitly referred to the frequency of the European Union's claim to be a model, when he stated: "It has been observed on many occasions that the European Union is one of the most successful examples of conflict resolution the world has known."[4] While it might be left to historians to inquire into the causal directions involved in European peace, the Franco-German rapprochement and economic integration, this claim is often a prelude to an argument that the European experience is transferable to other regions and that its normative basis is a proven case study on the linkages between democratisation, economic integration, sovereignty-pooling and peace-building.

Björn Hettne, one of the world's most authoritative experts on regionalism, highlights the contradictions involved in this conflation. He argues:

> The "second pillar" [of the original Treaty on European Union] is understood to encompass cooperation among the Member States in the foreign policy and security fields. It is mildly paradoxical that this cooperation is extremely sensitive and controversial, at the same time as the entire integration project is officially described as a historical peace project. Thus, security is described as the core of the EU project, but it seems instead to be an indirect effect of cooperation, which should not be seen in explicitly direct terms.[5]

Despite a healthy scepticism about the external foreign policy capacity of the EU, its role in creating inter-state peace is often left uncontested in comparative discussions about SAARC.[6] Even while the EU's external reach is dismissed, it is assumed to have played a central role in the sustaining of inter-state peace within its own borders.

The Development of EU Capacity for Conflict Resolution beyond its Borders since the European Security Strategy

The European Security Strategy was an attempt to put a strategic context on all EU activity with an impact on security, including areas such as aid, trade, immigration and police cooperation. Given that the threat of international terrorism has been identified as the number one threat to the EU, the implementation of European Security and Defence Policy (ESDP) ought to reflect the core concepts of the ESS. Beyond ESDP, other EU programmes and policy documents on security and development in particular should reflect some evidence of the integrated, coherent and multi-dimensional response set out in the ESS.

The role of ESDP in tackling international terrorism was first set out in detail one year after the ESS was agreed when the Council of Ministers adopted a "Conceptual Framework on the European Security and Defence Policy Dimension of the Fight Against Terrorism".[7] This policy framework closely followed the strategy's concept of security and the need for a broad range of responses. The detailed proposals in the document however focused only on ESDP and police cooperation issues which were narrowly defined. Action on prevention, for example, was limited to issues such as "information gathering and effective intelligence"[8] and not the wider issues of dealing with root causes in the 2003 European Security Strategy. Cooperation with NATO was mentioned but not cooperation with the United Nations. None of the action points identified could be regarded as dealing with the key areas, where the EU strategy document was identified as being different in focus from the US security strategy.

The EU Commission produced an overview document "Fight Against Terrorism" in 2005 which was written as an input into decisions by the Council but which set out in summary the key decisions and activity by the Commission itself and their proposals for future EU direction. In a 16-page input from the Commission to the debate on post-ESS responses to counter terrorism, the particular philosophy of the ESS was hardly visible.[9] The focus of the proposed work programme was on the criminal justice–terrorism overlap and not on issues around the underlying causes, or the connections between the sorts of regional conflicts which ESDP operations have focused on and security threats. The document dealt with border security, criminal law instruments, operational capacity (of law enforcement agencies), cooperation with the US, terrorist financing, transport security, critical infrastructure protection, customs and trade issues (totally focused on border protection without a mention of trade and development) and health security (focused on biological dangers not the threat of AIDS to human security). The potential of aid agreements to deal with root causes of conflict was briefly mentioned twice, but unlike in the criminal justice areas, there were no concrete proposals or action plans. This absence of any reflection of the wider concept of security policy set out in the ESS was particularly striking from the institution which has a particular role to play in policy coordination and coherence and which had direct responsibility for EU development aid and trade negotiations—two areas highlighted in the ESS as having an important role to play in EU security responses.

Subsequent documents from the Council of Ministers were equally narrow in their focus and also failed to reflect the multi-dimensional nature of EU security strategy set out in the ESS. The Council adopted policy conclusions on "security and development" in November 2007.[10] The document included a large focus on the need for coordination across different dimensions of EU activity, but apart from process issues and highly generalised statements, the only substantive issues addressed were security sector reform and working in humanitarian emergencies.[11] A Council document on the "Implementation of the Strategy and Action Plan to Combat Terrorism" in late 2008 began with some discussion on combating radicalisation but otherwise the exclusive focus of the 26-page overview document was on criminal justice, intelligence, border security and military and policing responses. Human rights were only discussed as a constraint on action, not as something linked to the creation of alienation and security threats. Neither was there any recognition of the linkages between regional conflicts or foreign policy in the Middle East and international security threats, as had been highlighted in the ESS.[12]

An ESDP "Factsheet" from 2007 had a slightly broader perspective.[13] The ESDP was portrayed as contributing "to improving the security environment which influences the conditions for violent radicalisation in third countries". Examples of ESDP activity of this type included the Aceh monitoring mission, the Rafah border monitoring and European Police Mission in Afghanistan (EUPOL). The document also highlighted EU aid projects in the field of good governance and the rule of law, which were "addressing factors which can contribute to radicalisation and recruitment". The focus of the rest of the short document was on criminal justice cooperation and military capacity-building, where the projects and programmes highlighted were much more specific. Another ESDP document on "external dimensions" mentioned development aid but only in the sense of adding "counter-terrorism clauses" to aid agreements and providing aid and technical assistance to countries lacking the capability to implement EU anti-terrorist requirements. There is not even a mention of using aid to deal with underlying causes.[14]

The European Commission continued to assert its involvement in crisis management, through both "rapid response" and long-term programmes, with the launch of its 'Instrument for Stability' (IfS) in 2007.[15] Crisis response projects under the Instrument for Stability focused on a wide range of issues, such as support for mediation efforts, confidence building, interim administrations, strengthening rule of law, transitional justice and the role of natural resources in conflict. Its first year budget was €91million and though the overview of this Commission programme did not explicitly mention it, the geographical focus was largely (but not exclusively) in areas where ESDP operations existed. For example, the Commission funded judicial reform programmes in Afghanistan, coinciding with the ESDP police mission; it supported security sector reform and reintegration projects in the Democratic Republic of Congo (DRC) and Guinea-Bissau, and a police training programme with the United Nations in Chad. The Commission also supported the international civilian office in Kosovo. While this was a new programme, at face value it had the potential to complement ESDP activities, but was funding long-term security reform and not projects aimed at the causes of conflict.

The worry for those involved in long-term development programmes is that rather than seeing the emergence of mutually supporting development and security policies, there is a securitisation of aid and development. The Commission's strategic planning and documentation around aid, development and security showed little evidence of structured integration. Within external relations and the new stability instrument the focus is on funding security projects. There is no discussion of the need to deal with underlying issues such as inequality and injustice as part of EU security policy. The launch of the second Commission security instrument in April 2009 was even more narrowly focused on proliferation of weapons of mass destruction and trans-regional crime. Other aspects of crisis response were limited to a programme to support NGO capacity-building. The Commission's statement on development cooperation addressed the security and development nexus from the other end of this divide, stating that "Addressing causes of conflicts (poverty, disease, lack of governance and rule of law) is an essential first step for the EU to help promote peace and development." However, while listed as an area of intervention, and an area where policy coherence is required, there was no active integration at the policy level of the underlying causes of conflict as identified in the security strategy. It was asserted that reducing poverty would assist in meeting security needs, but this was not developed or discussed in any meaningful way and beyond generalised platitudes and there was little evidence of a focus on the interactions between poverty and inequality and injustice which the international literature sees as central to the escalation of conflict.[16]

The key differences between the high-level discourse of the 2003 EU and 2002 US security strategies which dominated public and academic discussion in 2003 and 2004, were hardly visible at the lower level of Council and Commission policy implementation in the years which followed. The importance of dealing with root causes was occasionally mentioned but was not operationalised in any meaningful way in planning by either the Commission or the Council. There was no evidence in particular that dealing with injustice and inequality was built into security and development thinking in a manner which would see it reflected in practical projects. While at the level of discourse the European Security Strategy focused on multi-dimensional responses to security threats, at the policy implementation level this was narrowed to mean military, police and judicial cooperation. Trade and aid linkages to dealing with the causes of insecurity were entirely lost, other than using those areas as leverage, to get recipient states to implement specific counter-terrorist measures sought by the European Union.

Perhaps because they are easier to operationalise and because they were prioritised by security agencies, work programmes on security and development have dealt with security reform in developing states and not underlying causes of insecurity.

It is in the area of cooperation with the United Nations that the philosophy of the ESS was most visible. The ESDP has been firmly rooted within the UN system. Explicit UN security mandates were received for the vast majority of missions. Cooperation on the ground with the UN was reasonably good in most cases and improved over time. EU documents continued to repeat the importance of the UN's role in international security and this was also visible on the ground in how the Union worked. The willingness to look at alienation within European society which leads Europeans to support terrorism also stood out as a difference from the NSS.

Beyond this important difference of EU and US attitudes to the UN, an analysis of Commission and Council documents on security policy implementation showed that those elements in the ESS which were significantly different to the Bush Administration's National Security Strategy (NSS), were very rarely prioritised or at times even visible in EU decisions and documents. There was, in fact, remarkably little of the EU counter-terrorist and security material which would not with a slight change in rhetoric have fitted comfortably within the framework set out by the Bush Administration. The only clear exceptions to this were the constant references to UN mandates in the ESDP documents and the widespread positive references to the UN. There are some acknowledgements that there are root causes of conflict but policy priorities rarely addressed them.

There are of course some parallel decisions by the EU such as the commitment to higher development spending (at least to reach 0.7 per cent of EU GNP by 2015 in theory), a more balanced position on the Israeli–Palestinian conflict, and a commitment to a central role for the United Nations in international affairs, which run counter to the position in the 2002 American NSS. More generally, the EU was an active supporter of the Kyoto process on climate change and the International Criminal Court—both key high-profile issues within security and development. However, there was a very limited integration of these issues within the wider implementation of security policy. They were not developed into action items; there is no sense of these issues being prioritised or "mainstreamed" into policy responses.

The development of EU military operations since the launch of ESDP in 2003 initially showed a gradual increase in levels of activity and in the complexity of operations launched. From a very modest beginning in Macedonia in 2003, the Union moved in 2008 to undertake a challenging operation in Chad, simultaneous with its military commitments in Bosnia and while planning for its largest civilian mission in Kosovo. The logistical and command and control challenges set out during the capability-building phase in 1998-2003 were sufficiently met to allow the missions to proceed and meet their short-term objectives. The lack of EU capability in areas like air transport was not an insurmountable problem due to the nature of the missions but was a relatively serious issue in Chad, where the mobility and air support problems identified during the capacity-building phase were very evident, and the EU's military budget of nearly €200 million could not provide sufficient helicopters for a mission of 3,000 troops. This was partly resolved only by Russia joining the mission with a helicopter unit.

ESDP military missions have all had relatively limited aims, viz. bridging operations to allow the UN to get larger missions in place, election security, conflict prevention, post-conflict stabilisation and anti-piracy. While the environment was occasionally difficult and unstable, the level of military intensity was relatively low in all cases. Despite the very large focus on cooperation with NATO and the Berlin Plus arrangement and the build-up to the first operations, NATO facilities have, in fact, only been used in the operations in the Balkans where the EU took over the missions from NATO. All other military missions have used the national operational headquarters of a Member State. Interestingly, this has not just been a French choice, but was also done by Germany in the Congo and by Britain for the naval operation against Somali pirates.

On the civilian side, the EU began with a relatively challenging police mission in Bosnia, taken over from the United Nations. However, subsequently most other missions until Kosovo have been very small scale, some involving less than 20 deployed staff. A large number of ESDP missions have been essentially been of an advisory or training nature like those in DRC, Guinea-Bissau, Iraq and the first mission to Georgia. The monitoring missions in Aceh and Georgia, the police mission in Afghanistan and the border mission in Moldova have at least potentially been more challenging, with around 200 staff deployed on each. Security sector reform has been a significant focus of activity not only in the mission with that explicit aim but also, at least implicitly, in the policing missions.

For both military and civilian missions, there are clear geographical patterns to deployment. The EU neighbourhood has been very prominent with missions in the Balkans, Georgia and Moldova. Africa is increasingly the focus of activity, including four separate missions to the DRC. There has been no land-based deployment in a former British colony. Only two small missions were deployed in Palestine, despite its prominence in the ESS. The EU commitment in Aceh was related to the high-profile role of former Finnish President Marti Ahtisaari. The missions in Iraq and Afghanistan were relatively small ones (given the scale of security needs in both countries); the Iraq mission especially so. These missions can be seen as the EU making a gesture of conciliation to the United States without committing significant resources. The large-scale deployments in Kosovo and Bosnia—both on the EC's borders and both potential EU members—have been the most complex and the most expensive civilian missions, indicating the geopolitical influences on EU decisions about where to deploy. The limits of ESDP missions in Africa were reflected in the decision not to deploy a third military mission to northeast DRC in 2008, in the failure to deploy inside Darfur itself and in the limited nature of missions in Niger and Mali.

All ESDP missions except Macedonia and EULEX (European Union Rule of Law Mission) Kosovo had an explicit UN Security Council mandate. The absence of a UN mandate in Macedonia was due to Macedonia's recognition of Taiwan and had nothing to do with the mission itself.[17] The EULEX mission in Kosovo did not have an explicit Security Council resolution supporting it, because of Russia's position in support of Serbia, but it did operate under Resolution 1244 passed in 1999. This was stated in the Joint Action resolution from the Council of Ministers and was also asserted on the UN side by the UN Secretary General in a March 2009 report to the UN Security Council (UNSC). In the discussion on that report, Russia was critical of the EULEX mission, saying it was "far from status-neutral", meaning it supported state-building and independence for Kosovo.[18] The UNSC did however issue a Presidential statement in November 2008, with Russia's acquiescence welcoming the EU's efforts, but without explicitly mentioning EULEX.[19] None of the ESDP missions were politically controversial internationally. All of them were in keeping with the European Security Strategy's stated objectives of support for international law and the United Nations, and no individual operation caused significant political controversy either within the EU or internationally.

EU military missions under ESDP are still smaller than the EU's overall commitment to UN peacekeeping. The level of deployment of troops of EU Member States in UN peacekeeping operations is low (about 10 per cent of total UN troops deployed). It also has a very particular pattern; they have been overwhelmingly deployed in United Nations Interim Force in Lebanon (UNIFIL) (which was a largely EU-led operation after the 2006 Israel–Hezbollah conflict), on the Golan Heights (UN Disengagement Observer Force [UNDOF]), in Cyprus, and in Timor-Leste (where it is led by the former colonial power, viz. Portugal). There have been almost no EU troops on UN duty in Africa in recent years if you exclude those who stayed on when the EU mission in Chad shifted to UN control in March 2009. When the Irish army was deployed in Liberia from 2003 to 2007, they represented the largest military force from the EU deployed on UN duty in Africa. There is a low level of contribution from wealthy states to UN peacekeeping in Africa. The EU is the main reason why the United Nations has been a strong supporter of regional organisations taking on peace operations. If well-trained and well-equipped EU troops are more readily available for EU missions, because of Brussels' desire to project capability in this area, it may at least provide some additional resources for peacekeeping. Of course, this means that the United Nations does not have control over which countries it wants to deploy those well-equipped troops to. At present, however, they are not available in any case.

The first phase of ESDP operations was seen as a success largely because the EU was quite measured in what it had agreed to do. Former Director of the Stockholm International Peace Research Institute (SIPRI) Alison Bailes has argued that "it is hard to contend that the EU has chosen its missions on purely principled grounds such as the greatest humanitarian need, greatest benefit to the greatest number, greatest conformity with the principles of the EU Security Strategy and UN Charter".[20] The EU has a clear self-interest in security missions in its own neighbourhood. That is not to minimise the potential needs at the Union's borders, as the lack of action in Bosnia in the 1990s indicated, but the missions since 2003 have been of low intensity and have not escalated beyond what was planned for. The EU never had to radically adjust mission aims in the aftermath of deployment in response to a military challenge. Had the situation in the DRC escalated during the 2006 election it is not at all certain, given the reluctance within Germany to deploy, that the political will existed to put EU soldiers in the line of fire, and as no strategic reserve was provided it would have been difficult to respond with enough troops to dominate a volatile situation militarily. Bailes argued that the Union has not yet contemplated "a mission of the most strongly humanitarian sort that recognises an international 'responsibility to protect' in cases of genocide or severe abuse". Thus, it has yet to be tested to the limits of its ESDP commitments. In short, she adds: "A policy that dodges the challenge of cases like Darfur cannot call itself ethical just because it has not done anything blatantly non-ethical in other, more tractable cases".[21]

Finally, the challenge of launching ESDP within a coherent multi-dimensional security strategy as promised in the 2003 Document has largely not been met. The commitments have been repeated in EU discourse and no EU mission has been at odds with the vision of the strategy. However, there is little evidence that the promised focus on tackling underlying causes of insecurity such as injustice and inequality have been addressed in any serious fashion and beyond ESDP missions and individual projects; the focus has increasingly been on police, intelligence and criminal justice responses to security threats.

The EU and Conflict Resolution within its Borders

Northern Ireland

The Northern Ireland case is a good case study to explore the limits of impacts of the European Union conflict resolution with the EU itself since given its long duration, there were many opportunities for the European Economic Community (EEC)/ European Commission (EC)/EU to intervene. The conflict also varied over time in its intensity; it raised important issues of state responsibility for human rights abuses; it included an inter-state dimension, and finally saw a relatively successful peace process.[22] Potential EEC/EU interventions on Northern Ireland need to be explored within a wider international context of non-intervention during the Cold War as neither the United States nor the USSR for different reasons had any strategic desire to become involved. Just as Ireland was joining the then European Economic Community, Irish Foreign Minister and later Taoiseach (Prime Minister) Dr. Garret FitzGerald, who was a strong supporter of European integration, set out what he believed to be the most important potential influences of EEC membership on the Northern Ireland conflict and on wider relations between the Irish and British governments.[23] He believed that there would be a positive (if not dramatic) impact in a number of ways. At the ideological level, he thought it would strengthen a more cosmopolitan form of politics. At a functionalist level, he believed that it would promote north-south cooperation within Ireland on issues such as agriculture, which would then assist other more political developments. Finally, he argued that it would change the nature of sovereignty more generally and lower the direct relevance of competing ethno-nationalist claims in Northern Ireland. He did not seem to envisage any form of direct EC/EU involvement in the conflict. These four potential areas of impact, viz. ideological, direct intervention, functional and on the perceptions of sovereignty, provide a useful framework within which to explore the potential role of regional organisations in conflict resolution.

In brief, in the Northern Ireland case the impact of the EU has not been as significant as might have been assumed. There is no evidence of any significant change in national identity and political ideology in response to European integration. National identity in Northern Ireland is, arguably, stronger now than it was in 1973 and still divided almost entirely on Irish–British lines. While there were very important direct external interventions in the peace process, the EU as an institution was not involved, apart from as a funder after the ceasefires. The European Commission or the Council never took any formal decisions to intervene and the Parliament limited itself to a small number of human rights related resolutions.

Functionalist shifts in trade and shared decision-making on "non-constitutional" issues did not have the predicted impact of making cooperation less controversial before the ceasefires, but EU meetings did play a very important role in building a more normal working relationship between the Irish and British governments, their ministers and officials. The EU model may also have played a small role as an example in providing a model for post-Belfast or the Good Friday Agreement (1998) cross-border cooperation. Finally, the Union itself did not impact on UK conceptions of sovereignty during the conflict. However, there are parallel changes in the Belfast Agreement, where some more flexible conceptions of sovereignty are utilised in cross-border bodies and in the absence of requirements for declarations of loyalty to the state.

The Basque Country

The Northern Ireland experience is also not unique. The second most serious armed conflict within the EU borders, in the Basque country, saw an even more limited EU role. The Union could not even provide an informal forum since France never sought to play an active role. The Basques therefore had no access, even remotely, to this type of meeting. The Spanish state has been just as defensive of its absolute sovereignty on the matter as was the United Kingdom in Northern Ireland. This was re-enforced after the recent ETA (Euskadi Ta Askatasuna or Basque Homeland and Freedom) ceasefire when the Spanish state rejected absolutely any suggestion of an international monitoring group to confirm the ETA ceasefire. Therefore, even though the Union's role was limited it was more pronounced in Northern Ireland than in the Basque case. The Irish experience and indeed the Basque one within the EU where external intervention was even more limited, therefore, suggests that we should not set too high an ambition for SAARC in regional conflicts such as that in Kashmir.

The Contemporary European Context

The role of the Presidency has changed since the Lisbon Treaty came into effect and foreign and security policies issues are now more explicitly divided between the President of the European Council Herman von Rompuy, the former High Representative for Foreign Policy Catherine Ashton and the Council of Ministers. There was a lot of discussion about a single foreign and defence policy "phone number" in the discussions around a possible EU Constitution and what ultimately became the Lisbon Treaty; however the nature of the European Union is that, at least at this stage of its development, no such single source of power is possible. Control over EU foreign and defence policy *is* divided between EU institutions and Member States and among the states it is influenced both by the formal requirement for consensus among all states and the reality that larger states have more influence on such matters, even if they cannot on their own (even when such states are in agreement) move forward without the other smaller Member States.

While defence and security policy issues are divided between institutions, the European Council made up of Heads of Government/ Heads of State still represents a good reflection of EU political priorities at any point in time. From the adoption of the EU Security Strategy in 2003 through to December 2008 it received a report or held a discussion on European Security and Defence Policy (ESDP) as it was then termed, at almost every summit. As late as December 2008, as the financial crisis was deepening the European Council adopted a comprehensive declaration on ESDP.[24] After this point, however, the Common Security and Defence Policy drops off the European Council agenda as it becomes dominated by economic issues. Foreign policy issues with strong security focus are still discussed. For example, in March 2012, the Council agenda primarily dealt with the Eurozone crisis but there are agreed conclusions supporting democratic transition in the Middle East and North Africa, recognising the Syrian National Council, supporting the UN mission in Syria and support for "the Council, the Commission and the High Representative to maintain a comprehensive engagement with Somalia".[25] What is missing through all of this is any specific discussion on CSDP, or any possible military role which the EU as an institution might play. Looking back through 2010 and 2011, the same pattern can be seen. There are European Council discussions on Libya, Iran and Syria for example[26] and even quite significant diplomatic agreements, which in an earlier time might have been newsworthy in themselves. In June 2011, the European Council "confirms its full support for UN Security Council Resolutions 1970 and 1973 on Libya and for the efforts Member States of the EU are taking for their implementation".[27] It also "noted that the actions taken in conformity with the mandate from the Security Council significantly contributed to protecting civilians and civilian-populated areas under threat of attack and helped to save lives of civilians". Such broad-based support for military action which, even then, was not without its critics shows continuing political willingness to agree to common positions, but there is no evidence of a desire to involve the EU in military missions as an organisation, not even, to any significant degree in post-conflict situations.

In contrast to the strong focus from 2003 to 2008 on building EU military and civilian capacities to deal with a range of security challenges, from relatively unchallenging advice and monitoring missions, through rapid deployments such as Operation Artimus in the DRC and even relatively large-scale civilian missions such as Kosovo, the momentum of Common Security and Defence Policy (CSDP) from 2009-2010 onwards is very limited. Opportunities have presented themselves, but as NATO has struggled in Afghanistan, there was clearly little appetite among its European members for another significant international deployment and no one, at the time of writing, is seriously considering an intervention in Syria or Bahrain. While Operation Artimus in the DRC was an almost exclusively French affair, they sought to place it in an EU context. They did not feel the need to do that with Mali and while the Union will play a role it will be a much more limited one of training and capacity-building. Certainly the language of the European Security Strategy of 2003, is of the EU's potential strengths in multi-faceted operations with a military dimension, but with strong civilian elements drawing on development assistance, economic aid and support for post-conflict rebuilding (or conflict prevention) are still true. Perhaps the crisis in NATO makes the EU's case even stronger.

An analysis of the Council of Ministers meeting in its foreign affairs configuration with the Defence Minister twice a year, or even an analysis of specific documents on CSDP reinforces the impression provided by the lack of attention to CSDP at European Council level. In seems as if CSDP has reached a plateau. Current operations and some minor new ones can be agreed and financed without any political difficulty, but there seems to be no desire to mount a mission on the scale of the successful EUFOR mission in Chad, much less something even more challenging or long-term.

The context facing the EU's CSDP at present is one of remaining potential, but perhaps very limited ambition. The Battlegroups Concept is a case in point. Announced with fanfare as a major step forward in EU military capacity, we are now likely to reach the end of the first cycle of battlegroups without the concept ever being tested with an actual deployment. If Libya or Syria were never the situations envisaged by the European Security Strategy for EU deployment, South Sudan probably was. The mission to provide airport security, while not unimportant, is not the same as providing a border security force or a peace support force in the contested areas.

There is presently little pressure from Brussels for anything other than a status quo defence agenda. However, if the EU is to re-establish any momentum for an EU-specific security and defence policy with a strong focus on conflict resolution, then it needs to do more than providing merely diplomatic support for or remain silent on operations carried out by coalitions of the willing. It needs to re-energise the policy along the lines set out in the 2003 Security Strategy and to start a debate on what contribution the combined military forces of Member States, along with the civilian capacities built since 2003, might make under CSDP. Is the EU looking to play a role using its particular strengths for multi-faceted operations or is it content to play a minor role in global security in small largely civilian operations?

A Possible Agenda

CSDP needs to be re-invigorated if it is to survive as a credible operational force. The international security situation would benefit from an organisation with the resources and strong capacities for well integrated military and civilian peace support operations of the type envisaged during the capacity building phase of ESDP. In the context of an emerging multipolar world in the economic sphere at least, where does the EU wish to position itself in the security sphere? In a situation where NATO is still struggling to come to terms with its internal tensions and where it is clear that one of the significant reasons for the failure of the mission in Afghanistan was NATO's inability to integrate the political, diplomatic, civilian, developmental and mediation elements of the Afghan strategy—precisely those elements which the EU has a stated aim to perform well. A mission on the scale of Afghanistan is clearly not within the

EU's reach, but the lessons of NATO failure in Afghanistan are just as relevant for other smaller but equally complex missions.

There are two choices for the EU. A safe option would be status-quo focused. If the EU chooses that route, they will not face pressure to take any serious initiative. The cost at an EU level is that CSDP will be increasingly seen as a very minor initiative from a political union pre-occupied by its internal problems and which does not seek to play a role in the emerging world system beyond the economic arena. The lessons will not be lost on Brazil, Russia, India or China, or the G20 behind them. If global security interests are however seen as better protected by a strong EU, within a rules-based international system, based on the vision of security in the European Security Strategy then the EU needs to re-start a debate on the next phase of Common Security and Defence Policy.

Notes

1. Speech by European Affairs Minister Lucinda Creighton to the EMI/PAI Presidency Conference, "Ireland's Priorities for the EU Presidency," 18 April 2012, at http://www.merrionstreet.ie/index.php/2012/04/speech-by-european-affairs-minister-lucinda-creighton-to-the-emipai-presidency-conference-irelands-priorities-for-the-eu-presidency/.
2. *Dáil Debates*, 8 February 2002, 754(4),at http://debates.oireachtas.ie/dail/2012/02/08/00018.asp.
3. Article by Foreign Minister Guido Westerwelle published in the *Frankfurter Allgemeine Zeitung*, 14 December 2010, at http://www.nairobi.diplo.de/contentblob/2991522/Daten/1000100/BM_FAZ_Artikel141210_en.pdf, Other examples "Peace in the EU has become 'Normal', which is a Historic Success for the EU" (manifesto of European Greens 2006, at http://www.eurogreens.org/cms/default/dok/153/153995.a_green_future_for_europe@en.htm.
4. Statement by Irish Foreign Minister Brian Cowen at a Conference on the "Future of Europe after Enlargement", 11 October 2002, at http://www.dfa.ie/home/index.aspx?id=26206.
5. Björn Hettne, "Regional Actorship and Regional Agency: Comparative Perspectives," Paper at 6th Garnet PhD School, Brussels, 9-13 June 2008. "Global Governance & Regionalism: The Institutional Dimension", p. 8. http://www.garnet-eu.org/fileadmin/documents/phd_school/6th_phd_school/Professors_papers/Hettne.pdf
6. Hasan-Askari Rizvi, "SAARC: Problems of Regional Cooperation," *South Asian Studies* (Lahore), vol. 13, 2006, pp. 125-141.
7. http://ue.eu.int/uedocs/cmsUpload/ESDPdimension.pdf. Adopted 2 November 2004.

8. Para 12 and 13.
9. EU Commission *Fight Against Terrorism (Sec 332)*, 2005.
10. http://ec.europa.eu/development/icenter/repository/council_conclusions_security_development_15097_en.pdf
11. Ibid.
12. Report to Council, 19 November 2008. http://www.consilium.europa.eu/uedocs/cmsUpload/st15912.en08.pdf A separate document covering an earlier period is even narrower focusing almost exclusively in tracking criminal justice and anti-terror legislation. http://register.consilium.europa.eu/pdf/en/08/st15/st15912-ad01re01.en08.pdf
13. http://ue.eu.int/uedocs/cmsUpload/Factsheet-fight%20against%20terrorism%20ENMarch2007.pdf#_
14. http://ue.eu.int/showPage.aspx?id=1412&lang=En
15. http://ec.europa.eu/external_relations/ifs/index_en.htm
16. See, for example, Christopher Cramer, "Does Inequality Cause Conflict?," *Journal of International Development*, 15, 2003, pp. 397-412 and Karen Ballentine and Jake Sherman, eds., *The Political Economy of Armed Conflict: Beyond Greed and Grievance* (Boulder, CO: Lynne Rienner, 2003).
17. This led to a decision by the Irish Government not to take part, in strict conformity with their requirement for UN Security Council approval.
18. Record of UNSC meeting, 23 March 2009, p. 14. http://daccessdds.un.org/doc/UNDOC/PRO/N09/276/20/PDF/N0927620.pdf?OpenElement.
19. http://daccessdds.un.org/doc/UNDOC/GEN/N08/622/50/PDF/N0862250.pdf?OpenElement.
20. Alyson J. K. Bailes, "The EU and a 'Better World': What Role for the European Security and Defence Policy?" *International Affairs*, 84(1), 2008, p. 123.
21. Ibid., p. 124.
22. For some background on the Northern Ireland case see John Doyle, "Governance and Citizenship in Contested States: The Northern Ireland Peace Agreement as Internationalised Governance," *Irish Studies In International Affairs*, 10, 1999, pp. 201-219 and John Doyle, "Re-examining the Northern Ireland Conflict," in Vassilis K. Fouskas, ed., *Politics of Conflict: A Survey* (London: Routledge, 2007), pp. 132-146.
23. Garret FitzGerald, *Towards a New Ireland*, (London: Charles Knight and Co, 1972).
24. European Council Conclusions, 11-12 December 2008. http://consilium.europa.eu/uedocs/cms_data/docs/pressdata/en/ec/104692.pdf.
25. European Council Conclusion, 1-2 March 2012. http://register.consilium.europa.eu/pdf/en/12/st00/st00004-re02.en12.pdf , pp. 11-13
26. European Council Conclusions, December 2011. http://www.consilium.europa.eu/uedocs/cms_data/docs/pressdata/en/ec/126714.pdf.
27. European Council Conclusions, 23-24 June 2011. http://www.consilium.europa.eu/uedocs/cms_data/docs/pressdata/en/ec/123075.pdf.

4
The European Union and Conflict Resolution in Afghanistan

Gulshan Sachdeva

Introduction

The conflict in Afghanistan could determine the nature of the future security architecture in Asia, which is still evolving. With ambitions in the field of global conflict management, the European Union and its Member States have made significant contributions to military, development and reconstruction activities in Afghanistan. European involvement in Afghanistan will also have implications for Europe as a credible security actor in global operations. As a conflict manager, the Union's activities in the last two decades have taken place against the background of the development of the concept of comprehensive security,[1] which makes it necessary for the EU and its Member States to coordinate their respective military and civilian strengths in different phases of the conflict. At the same time, the "Big Members" needed to coordinate their actions among themselves and with the institutions in Brussels.[2] The 1993 Maastricht Treaty, the *European Security Strategy* (2003) and the Lisbon Treaty (2009) provide a framework for EU conflict resolution and explicitly called upon the Union to engage in the full range of conflict resolution activities.[3] In Afghanistan, the Union's development efforts are being supplemented by the military, economic and diplomatic contributions of its Member States. The Afghan conflict has shown some European strengths, especially in the areas of reconstruction, institution building and conflict negotiation. It has also revealed the limited value of the EU notions of conflict resolution when dealing with "out of area" operations and when other major players like the United States are in a dominating position to set the "conflict resolution" agenda. To some extent, the visibility and effectiveness of the Union has suffered from the lack of coordination among its Member States and institutional incoherence.[4]

Understanding the Afghanistan Project

In the last four decades, Afghanistan has witnessed diverse projects of nation-building and socio-political transformation. The Soviet project of building communism in Afghanistan resulted in over a million dead and five million Afghan refugees, mainly in the neighbourhood. Similarly, when Pakistan pushed the conservative Taliban regime in Afghanistan, the world faced disastrous consequences, including the 9/11 terrorist attacks on the United States. The current international project of building democracy and market economy is mandated by the United Nations and is being mainly implemented by the Western alliance led by the United States. More than 70 nations have committed resources for Afghan reconstruction with the United States being the biggest donor. Moreover, many European and Asian countries have also committed significant resources. A major portion of these resources have gone into building the Afghan National Army, the Afghan Police as well as a variety of education, health, community development projects and institutions of governance. These projects have led to major gains being made in education, health, infrastructure, economic development as well as in women empowerment, which needs to be consolidated. These gains have been made despite the difficult and deteriorating security situation in many parts of the country.

State Building

Decades of war, followed by the Taliban regime, destroyed the core institutions of the Afghan state. The heavily war-torn economy faced high levels of absolute poverty, ill health, large-scale illiteracy and complete marginalisation of women. Moreover, millions of Afghans left the country and became refugees mainly in the neighbouring countries. After the fall of the Taliban, all Afghan factions which were opposed to the Taliban attended a meeting in Bonn in December 2001, which was sponsored by the United Nations. The Bonn agreement[5] charted the roadmap for the political transformation of the country into a democratic state. The UN Security Council endorsed the agreement through its Resolution 1383.[6] Under the leadership of Hamid Karzai, a Transitional Administration was established to guide the process of transformation. The interim administration derived its authority through the *Loya Jirga* (Grand Council) convened by former Afghan King Zahir Shah. In early 2002, international donors pledged about $4.5 billion in Tokyo for reconstruction efforts in Afghanistan. In March 2002, the UN also established the UN Assistance Mission in Afghanistan (UNAMA). The constitutional *Loya Jirga* adopted a new constitution in January 2004, with a presidential form of government. In April 2004 in Berlin, 23 donor nations pledged a total of $8.2 billion aid to Afghanistan over three years.[7] Under the new constitution, presidential elections were held in October 2004 and parliamentary elections in September 2005. More than 75 per cent voters participated in the presidential election and a significant number of women to the National Assembly were elected. The constitution also established legal protection for the private property and it was presumed that economic development in the country will be based mainly on the market economy. These were remarkable achievements for a country destroyed by decades of war.

Once these landmarks were achieved, the international community and the Afghan government agreed on the *Afghanistan Compact*[8] at the London Conference in 2005. The compact set ambitious targets for security, governance, development, regional cooperation and counter-narcotics. While reviewing the Afghanistan Compact, at another international conference on Afghanistan in Paris in June 2008, the international community made further commitments for the next five years.[9] Despite serious difficulties, the process of a second presidential as well as parliamentary elections has also been completed. The new "Afghanistan–Pakistan Regional Stabilization Strategy" outlined by the US State Department in January 2010 focused on the reintegration, expanded civilian presence and regional diplomacy. At the London Conference (28 January 2010), participants "re-affirmed the goals of greater Afghan leadership, increased regional cooperation and more effective international partnership".[10] To end the stalemate, the international community is also broadly in favour of the process of reconciliation and reintegration. Subsequently, in July 2010, the Kabul Conference initiated the so-called "Kabul Process" of transition to full Afghan leadership and responsibility. It was agreed that the "Afghan National Security Forces (ANSF) should lead and conduct military operations in all provinces by the end of 2014".[11]

At the Bonn and Istanbul conferences in 2011, both the international community as well as regional players re-affirmed their long-term commitment to the future of Afghanistan, which goes much beyond 2014. The Bonn Conference (December 2011) was attended by 85 countries and 15 international organisations. At the conference, all participants dedicated themselves to "deepening and broadening their historic partnership from Transition to the Transformation Decade of 2015-2024".[12] The final declaration talked about mutual commitments in the areas of governance, security, the peace process, economic and social development and regional cooperation. Earlier, in November 2011 at the Istanbul Conference which was attended by the so-called "Heart of Asia" countries consisting of Afghanistan, China, India, Iran, Pakistan, Russia, Saudi Arabia, Turkey, the UAE and all Central Asian republics, participants reaffirmed their strong commitment to a "secure, stable and prosperous Afghanistan in a secure and stable region". The regional participants, among other things, in the context of Afghanistan, also agreed to respect the territorial integrity of states; non-intervention in the internal affairs of other states; dismantling terrorist sanctuaries and safe havens; disrupting all financial and tactical support for terrorism and support for the stability and peace in Afghanistan, as well as respect for Afghanistan's sovereignty, unity and territorial integrity. At the Tokyo conference in July 2012, donors agreed to provide $16 billion over the next four years. Moreover, American officials also talked about working for a New Silk Road Strategy for Afghanistan.

European Engagement in Afghanistan

The current international state-building project is mandated by the United Nations and is being implemented mainly by the Western alliance led by the United States. More than 70 nations have committed over US$ 90 billion for Afghan reconstruction. Through the end of 2011, the United States has pledged US$67 billion, out of which a significant portion has already been disbursed.[13] About 50 per cent of this aid had gone into building the Afghan National Army and the Afghan National Police. Other commitments are in the areas of economic and social development, governance, counter-narcotics and support to many civil society activities. These figures do not include resources provided for US troops serving in Afghanistan. Altogether, it is estimated that in the last one decade, the American taxpayers have provided about $443 billion to the war in Afghanistan.[14]

The second most substantial commitment to Afghanistan is from Europe. Individual EU Member States and the European Commission are making a significant contribution to security and justice reforms, development and reconstruction, counter-narcotics and regional cooperation activities in Afghanistan. The European Union is also involved in security sector reform[15] and has deployed a police mission. According to EU official sources, it committed about €2.5 billion assistance to Afghanistan between 2002 and 2011. By the end of 2011, it had already disbursed more than €2 billion (about 85 per cent) of the committed funds (see Table 1). This assistance from the EU budget is managed by the EU Delegation in Kabul. The framework for this cooperation is governed by *Country Strategy Paper* (CSP) and *Multiannual Indicative Programme* (MIP) formally agreed with the Afghan Government. In the *Country Strategy Paper 2007-2013*, resources are earmarked for six areas, three focal and three non-focal:

Table 1: EU Aid to Afghanistan, 2002-2011 (in € million)

Year	Total Commitments	Disbursed
2002	248	151
2003	286	214
2004	247	171
2005	224	206
2006	201	176
2007	196	225
2008	214	213
2009	270	286
2010	255	215
2011	347	261
Total	**2488**	**2118**

Source: European Commission, *European Union, Afghanistan, State of the Play*, July 2012. **Focal Areas**: Governance, Rural Development, Health
Non Focal Areas: Social Protection, Mine Action, Regional Cooperation

Out of € 610 million agreed for MIP for the period 2007-2010, €542 million were used in three focal areas namely governance (42 per cent), rural development (28 per cent) and health (20 per cent). The balance was earmarked for social protection (3.9 per cent), de-mining activities (3.6 per cent) and regional cooperation (3.6 per cent). Similarly for the *MIP 2011-2013*, the proposed breakup was 35.8 per cent on rural development, 20.8 per cent on health and 0.8 per cent on social protection, about 40 per cent on governance and rule of law (police reform, public administrative reform, justice reforms); and about 2.5 per cent on regional cooperation.

Table 2: Multiannual Indicative Programme, 2011-2013

Priority Areas/sectors		Projected			% of MIP
		2011	2012	2013	
Rural Development	Local Development			105	35.8%
	Agriculture		60	50	
	Sub Total				**215**
Social Sector	Health		125		20.6 %
	Social Protection		5		+ 0.8 %
	Sub Total				**130**
Governance and Rule of Law	Police Reform	140	30		
	Sub-national Governance			10	
	Public Administration Reform	40			**40%**
	Justice Reform	20			
	Sub-Total				**240**
Non-focal	Regional cooperation			15	*2.5%*
Total		**200**	**220**	**180**	*600*

Source: European Commission, *European Union, Afghanistan, State of the Play*, July 2012.

According to data released by the Government of Afghanistan together with the EU, European nations had committed about around $12 billion for reconstruction activities for the period between 2002 and 2011.

Table 3: European Assistance to Afghanistan, 2002-2011 (Commitments)

	Amount (US$ Million)		Amount (US$ Million)
European Union	2883	United Kingdom	2222
Germany	2130	Netherlands	1015
Norway	775	Italy	645
Sweden	635	Denmark	438
France	323	Spain	220
Finland	160	Switzerland	118
Czech republic	108	Belgium	61
Ireland	22	Poland	22
Luxembourg	12	Hungary	6
Lithuania	6	Austria	5
		Total	**11806**

Source: Afghanistan, Ministry of Finance, *Development Cooperation Report 2010* (Kabul: 2010), p. 96.

Moreover, 25 out of 27 EU Member States have participated in the North Atlantic Treaty Organization (NATO)-led International Security Assistance Force (ISAF) mission. By the beginning of December 2012, about 28,000 troops from the EU Member States were serving in Afghanistan. Major contributing nations include the UK (9,500), Germany (4,316), Italy (4,000), Poland (1,770), Spain (1,606), Romania (1,549), Bulgaria (581), Denmark (567), Hungary (582), France (543), the Netherlands (500), the Czech Republic (416) and Sweden (413).

On reconstruction, the United Kingdom has spent about $2.222 billion and has also been a lead nation in counter-narcotics programmes. The Germans have provided resources worth more than $2 billion. It was the lead nation for police reform before it was transferred to the European Union Police Mission in Afghanistan (EUPOL) in 2007. In an integrated approach, the Netherlands believed that defence, development and diplomacy are crucial for achieving peace and stability. It spent about $1.015 billion till

2011. Compared to the Dutch and German approach, the French Government focuses more on security. The Italian involvement is low key and more restricted. It has also focused on strengthening the judicial system.

Despite significant improvements in some of these areas, public opinion within Europe remains skeptical about their countries' involvement in Afghanistan. Even before President Barrack Obama's speech on 22 June 2011, in which he announced the American drawdown, many European governments were under pressure to reduce or end their military mission. When the Obama Administration indicated that they would be winding up the mission in 2014, most European nations have indicated that they will also be ending their military mission in 2014.

Overall, it is not an easy task to conclude what European policy-makers agree on Afghanistan. Still, as Daniel Korski aptly remarks, they seem to agree on "the opening of negotiations with 'reconcilable' Taliban insurgents, more civilian reconstruction, a development-based approach to counter-narcotics, more training for the Afghan security forces to enable them to lead the counter-insurgency effort, and regional initiatives that include not only Pakistan but also India, Iran and China".[16]

Afghanistan beyond 2014

Apart from broad discussions on 2014 drawdown by international forces, developments in the last two years, including the assassination of Ustad Burhanuddin Rabbani in September 2010, speculations on negotiations with the Taliban, on-going regional anxieties and continuing global economic crisis have pointed towards increasing unpredictability about Afghanistan's future. Besides, the tensions between the US and Pakistan and instability within Pakistan have further complicated future scenarios for Afghanistan.

An important reason for this uncertainty is that almost everyone involved in the Afghanistan project believes that by 2014 a significant number of coalition forces would have left the country, even if some

American forces continue to stay for longer periods mainly in non-combat missions. In June 2011, President Obama announced that American policies had already accomplished most major goals and that the drawdown of 33,000 US troops would start by September 2012. Despite doubts about the durability, the transition to Afghan leadership began as planned, in July 2011, and is continuing. The security responsibility for many provinces and cities has already been handed over to Afghan authorities.

Although this transition has already begun, it is quite obvious to all that due to the weak Afghan government and safe havens for insurgents in Pakistan, the country will still need direct security assistance even after 2014. As a result, the Afghan Government has concluded "strategic partnerships" with a number of countries including the United States, India, the United Kingdom, Germany and France. All have committed resources for the transition and transformational decade. It is hoped that American troops that will remain in Afghanistan will come under the auspices of the Bilateral Security Agreement (BSA). Negotiations on the BSA were concluded and an agreement was sent to President Hamid Karzai to sign in late 2013. However, he refused to sign on the ground that it would be more appropriate for his successor to sign it. Broadly, the political community in Afghanistan is in favour of the BSA as it was also approved by the *Loya Jirga* in November 2013. Both presidential candidates, viz. Abdullah Abdullah and Ashraf Ghani, have publicly supported the security agreement. Overall, post-2014 Afghanistan is going to face three major challenges—security, political and developmental. The security situation in Afghanistan has deteriorated significantly since 2007 and will remain difficult in the foreseeable future. With the drawdown of foreign forces, the situation will become even more challenging for the Afghan administration.

In 2011, the Joint Coordination and Monitoring Board (JCMB), which is responsible for overall strategic coordination between the Afghan Government and the international community, reached an agreement to increase the Afghan National Police Force from

134,000 to 157,000 and the Afghan National Army from 171,000 to 195,000. Although these numbers have already increased significantly, the security forces will need much more mentoring than provided so far. Due to higher rates of desertion, many more also need to be trained on a regular basis. The Americans have so far provided a major share of resources for training. In fact, about 50 per cent of their committed and disbursed resources for reconstruction and development in Afghanistan have gone only to train security forces. The Europeans have already made some contributions for police training. Apart from the lack of socio-cultural understanding of new Afghan soldiers, Western training has also been very expensive.

Another major challenge faced by Afghanistan is at the economic front. With declining Western interest, the amount of resources available for development projects in the next decade is likely to be significantly lower than the previous one. Experience suggests that withdrawal of international troops in other parts of the world have led to a reduction of civilian aid, with implications for economic growth and fiscal sustainability. Therefore, potential financing gaps in the budget could threaten security and recent progress made at the developmental front. According to the World Bank, actual aid to Afghanistan in 2010-11 was about $16 billion, about the size of the nominal GDP.[17] According to the *Asian Development Bank Outlook 2011*, the planned foreign troop pullout by 2014 may lower growth by at least 2-3 percentage points.[18] Any rapid decline in aid will severely affect growth performance and the employment scenario in the country. The *ADB Outlook 2014* shows that growth in GDP excluding opium production has already declined to 3.3 per cent in 2013. This was much below the 12 per cent growth achieved in 2012. Despite international commitment for the 'transformation decade', the Afghan government will be forced to deploy its limited resources on maintaining security infrastructure.

In late 2011, former US Ambassador to Afghanistan and Iraq, Zalmay Khalilzad, predicted that what happens in 2014 and beyond would depend on the success and failure of the American strategy regarding the elimination of terrorist sanctuaries in the region; catalysing a strategic shift in Pakistan policy from supporting those who are fighting NATO and Afghan forces—the Taliban, the Haqqani network and others—to facilitating a political settlement in Afghanistan; persuading the Afghan Government to deal with issues concerning governance and corruption; and pursuing a positive outlook for the region based on economic integration and the establishment of a New Silk Road.[19]

Whatever the United States does, none of its policies is likely to deliver conclusive results by 2014. Another European and the American strategy has been of some kind of reconciliation with the Taliban. In the last two years, there have been many reports indicating some movement in this matter. Many European nations, particularly the British and German governments have been quite active in promoting these talks. However, the problem with this strategy, as Henry Kissinger noted recently, is that "If you negotiate while your forces are withdrawing, you're not in a great negotiating position."[20] It is clear that Afghanistan will need some kind of political settlement at some time in future. However, recent developments seem like a desperate attempt by some European nations as part of the "exit strategy" rather than an important element of a long-term nation-building process in Afghanistan.

Conclusion

In the last decade, Afghanistan has made significant gains in infrastructure, education, health, economic development and women empowerment, which need to be consolidated. The current security situation in the country is serious but not hopeless. The only possible way is to increase the numbers and capabilities of Afghan security forces, put pressure on anti-government forces and also continuously work for political solutions. It is also evident that despite major challenges, Afghanistan has the potential to play an important role in facilitating regional integration for different economies of South and Central Asia. If proposals concerning regional economic cooperation originating from Afghanistan are implemented by other countries in the region, this could ultimately improve chances of peace not only between India and Pakistan but also in the entire Eurasian region.

The successful completion of two rounds of presidential elections shows the extent to which European analysts were wrong in predicting future scenarios concerning Afghanistan. Many thought that the country's leaders are preparing for a civil war. Many observers were fully convinced that the solution to Afghanistan's problem was largely dependent on working out some kind deal with the Taliban. A lot of energy and resources in the last three years were wasted on the so called "reconciliation process" with very little results. The real reconciliation is happening now, not through some shady deals by foreign powers behind the scene but through the widespread participation by all sections of the society in the democratic process. The process indicates that ordinary Afghan citizens, who have seen some fruits of development in the last decade and have seen their kids going to school, are looking much beyond ethnic divisions. This also shows the increasing capabilities of Afghan security forces.

Recent discussions on Afghanistan indicate that in the post-2014 phase, the country is going to face three major challenges—security, political and economic. In all three areas, European engagement could help the country meet these difficult challenges during its decade of transformation. Apart from reconstruction activities, the EU and its Member States are likely to be active in reconciliation efforts as well as in promoting some kind of a "regional solution". So far European efforts in Afghanistan have met with limited success. Many of the developmental efforts have not been possible due to the deteriorating security situation in the last few years. Although the European concept emphasises on comparative advantage in the comprehensive approach, Lt. Gen. Karl Eikenberry, who had first-hand experience of European efforts in Afghanistan, is critical of the progress it has made in "developing the truly expeditionary, non-military capability essential to delivering the comprehensive approach in expeditionary environments". Secondly, he asks: "If Europe has an advantage in the comprehensive approach, why does the EU compartmentalize its military and civilian sides?"[21] Nevertheless, given the complexity of the situation in Afghanistan, European achievements cannot be underestimated. However, this also indicates limitations of the EU concept of conflict resolution. Moreover, any conflict resolution effort has to find a long-lasting solution to the root cause of the problem. And in the case of Afghanistan where the root of the problems are in Pakistan, many of the efforts within Afghanistan will always be of limited value.

Notes

1. Carmen Gebhard and Per Martin Norheim-Martinsen, "Making Sense of EU Comprehensive Security towards Conceptual and Analytical Clarity," *European Security*, 20(2), 2011, pp. 221-241.
2. Richard G Whitman and Stefan Wolff, eds., *The European Union as a Conflict Manager* (London: Routledge, 2012).
3. Nathalie Tocci, "The EU in Conflict Resolution," in Stefan Wolff and Christalla Yakinthou, eds., *Conflict Resolution: Theories and Practice* (London: Routledge, 2011).
4. Eva Gross, "The EU in Afghanistan," in Richard G Whitman and Stefan Wolff, eds., *The European Union as a Conflict Manager* (London: Routledge, 2012), p. 107.5.
5. For text of Bonn Agreement, see *Agreement on Provisional Arrangements in Afghanistan Pending the Re-establishment of Permanent Government Institutions*, available at http://unama.unmissions.org/Portals/UNAMA/Documents/Bonn-agreement.pdf (accessed on 1 July 2010).
6. See UN Security Council Resolution number 1383, 6 December 2001, available at http://daccess-ods.un.org/TMP/5722597.html (accessed on 6 July 2010).
7. See *Berlin Declaration*, available at http://reliefweb.int/rw/rwb.nsf/db900SID/SNAO-634SXS?OpenDocument (accessed on 6 July 2011).
8. See *Afghanistan Compact*, available at http://unama.unmissions.org/Portals/UNAMA/Documents/AfghanistanCompact-English.pdf (accessed on 15 September 2011).
9. See *Paris Declaration*, 12 June 2008, available at http://unama.unmissions.org/Portals/UNAMA/Documents/Paris-con-Declaration-English.pdf (accessed on 20 September 2011).
10. Communiqué of *Afghanistan: The London Conference* http://unama.unmissions.org/Default.aspx?ctl=Details&tabid=1741&mid=1882&ItemID=7521 (accessed on 10 October 2011).
11. http://unama.unmissions.org/Portals/UNAMA/Documents/Kabul%20Conference%20Communique.pdf (accessed on 10 October 2011).
12. Bonn Conference Conclusions, Afghanistan and the International Community: From Transition to the Transformation Decade, 5 December 2011, http://www.auswaertiges-amt.de/cae/servlet/contentblob/603686/

publicationFile/162662/Konferenzschlussfolgerung_engl.pdf.

13. Kenneth Katzman, *Afghanistan: Post-Taliban Governance, Security, and U.S. Policy* (Washington: Congressional Research Service), 22 September 2011, http://www.fas.org/sgp/crs/row/RL30588.pdf (accessed on 8 October 2011).
14. Ibid.; also see Benjamin D Hopkins and Magnus Marsden, "Ten Years In, Afghan Myths Live On," *The New York Times*, 7 October 2011.
15. Eva Gross, *Security Sector Reform in Afghanistan: The EU's Contribution*, Occasional Paper No. 78 (Paris: European Union Institute for Security Studies, 2009).
16. Daniel Korski, *Shaping Europe's Afghan Surge*, Policy Brief No 11, European Council on Foreign Relations, March 2009, p. 3.
17. *Transition in Afghanistan: Looking Beyond 2014* (Washington, DC: The World Bank, 2011).
18. Asian Development Bank, *Asian Development Outlook* (Manila: ADB, 2011), p. 157.
19. Zalmay Khalilzad, Testimony to House Committee on Foreign Affairs, "2014 and Beyond: U.S. Policy towards Afghanistan and Pakistan, Part I," 3 November 2011.
20. Henry A. Kissinger, "Talk to Afghan Neighbors," http://www.politico.com/news/stories/1111/67384.html.
21. Lieutenant-General Karl Eikenberry, "Europe and Conflict Resolution: Isolated or Engaged?", Address to the IISS Global Strategic Review, Geneva, 14 September 2008.

5
The European Union and Conflict Resolution in Nepal

Manish Thapa

At the beginning of the twenty-first century, the European Union stands out as an important regional organisation. It entertains formalised relations with almost all other (groups of) states. Although much of its attention is devoted to internal integration, the Union cannot and does not wish to be an isolated entity. Instead it has expressed the desire and ambition to take up a prominent place in the contemporary world order. In addition to the general goal of forging good relations with (potential) political and economic partners across the globe, the Union also wishes to use its place in international relations as a vehicle for advocating some of the values it considers important. Among these values are democracy, social welfare, human rights and liberalism. One of the key aspects of European foreign policy is to contribute in manifold ways to peace support operations. The European Commission has a strong external relations *acquis* in projecting peace abroad, notably in the form of preventive diplomacy and long-term civilian peace-building.[1]

The European Commission's assistance to Nepal dates back to 1977. In June 1996, the EC–Nepal Framework Cooperation Agreement came into force, outlining the general conditions for providing technical assistance and cooperation. The principal objectives of this Agreement were to enhance and develop the various aspects of cooperation between the Parties. EC's assistance to Nepal during the period 2007-2013 had an estimated budget of €120 million and focused on three areas, viz. education (with human rights, conflict prevention and good governance and related issues); stability and peace-building and trade facilitation and economic capacity-building.[2] To further consolidate its effort, the European Union on 8 July 2011 agreed to provide a grant assistance of €22 million for the implementation of the Support for Stability and Peace Building Programme. Thus, peace-building and conflict resolution is one of the key priority areas of assistance from the European Commission to Nepal. This chapter outlines the European Union's support to conflict resolution initiatives and its implications on the conflict resolution process of Nepal.

The European Union and Conflict Resolution

The Treaty on the European Union explicitly states that the Union's aim is to promote peace (Article 3(1)) and that its role in the world should reflect the principles that have inspired its creation, development and enlargement (Article 21(1), first subparagraph). The Treaty identifies the preservation of peace, the prevention of conflict and the strengthening of international security among the Union's core foreign policy priorities (Article 21(2)(c)). More interestingly, the EU's conception of peace, which has been elaborated since the 1990s, has been broad, long-term and organic, and has included the principles of democracy, human rights, the rule of law, international law, good governance and economic development.[3] This conception is tied to that of peace-building, which is embedded within the tradition of the "liberal peace" and can be traced back to former UN Secretary General Boutros Boutros-Ghali's 1992 "Agenda for Peace". In other words, as the EU emerged as a foreign policy actor engaged in conflict resolution in the 1990s, it espoused and elaborated the goal of peace-building. This goal has been in line both with the Union's intrinsic nature and ethos as well as with the approach developed by the United Nations in those years.

These public pronouncements clearly suggest that the EU's commitment is to long-term conflict resolution rather than short-term engagements. Although with the development of the Common Security and Defense Policy (CSDP), the European Union has deployed a number of civilian and military missions in conflicts worldwide—these have been typically aimed at medium-to-long term aims such as border monitoring, security sector reform and judicial reform. In other words, the EU is not simply interested in pursuing the management of crises and conflicts through the maintenance of ceasefires and the negotiation of political settlements. It rejects the idea that violent conflict is endemic to human nature and espouses the view that conflict resolution and transformation is possible through the search for mutually beneficial solutions that allow for the satisfaction of the basic human needs of all parties.[4] Moreover, the Union regards elements such as human and minority rights, democracy, state legitimacy, dispute-resolution mechanisms, the rule of law, social solidarity, sustainable development and a flourishing civil society to be critical "indicators" of conflict prevention and conflict resolution.[5] This suggests that the Union aims at transforming the structural features of violent conflict, eradicating what Johan Galtung[6] defined as the seeds of structural violence, viz. social injustice, unequal development and discrimination. While theoretically distinct, the EU's approach also fits in with what Oliver Richmond[7] conceptually and more broadly defines as third-generation "peace-building approaches", which cover the wider economic, political and social make-up of countries before, during and after the end of violent conflict.

Beyond foreign policy objectives, the EU is also endowed with policy instruments, which are particularly well suited to pursuing conflict resolution and peace-building. Alongside the sphere of the Common Foreign and Security Policy (CFSP), the Union promotes conflict resolution principally through its "constructive engagement" with conflict parties.[8] By constructive engagement, EU actors mean the deployment of a wide variety of measures of cooperation, which are normally specified in contractual agreements with third countries. These contractual relations take different forms, providing for different degrees of integration in, and cooperation with, the European Union. They range from the accession process aiming at the full membership of a candidate country to looser forms of association, which envisage measures of economic, political and social cooperation with EU structures, to trade and development agreements with African–Caribbean and Pacific countries. These looser forms of association are also "contractual" in nature. Rather than a treaty of accession as in the case of the accession process, they foresee association agreements, partnership and cooperation agreements, stabilisation and association agreements, etc. Beyond the goal of achieving varying degrees of cooperation with the EU, these contractual ties aim at fostering long-term structural change, such as conflict resolution, within and between third countries.

The Engagement of the European Commission in Nepal, 1975-2006

The European Commission is one of the major donors of Nepal since the mid-1970s. Since diplomatic relations were established, most of the European Commission's aid has been directed towards improving the infrastructure in remote areas.[9]

The European Commission established diplomatic relations with Nepal in 1975 and development assistance began as early as 1977 in areas like irrigation and watershed management, animal health, reproductive health, primary education, refugees and institutional capacity-building. The EC–Nepal Cooperation Agreement was signed on 20 November 1995 covering the following areas: respect for human rights and democratic principles, cooperation in trade, development, science and technology, energy, agriculture, the environment, and action to combat drugs and HIV and AIDS.

The 2002-2006 European Commission strategy supported development efforts as defined in the Agenda of Priority Reform Actions and the Poverty Reduction Strategy Papers (PRSP) Five Year Plan (2002-2007).[10] The Commission provided support to the poverty reduction agenda with support for economic development through agriculture development, social sector development, targeted programmes, good governance and decentralisation.[11] Several EU

Member States have also established bilateral relationships with Nepal and are playing an active role as important development partners of Nepal. Five of them have established individual diplomatic missions in Kathmandu, viz. Denmark, Finland, France, Germany and the United Kingdom.[12]

The Commission's Technical Office in Nepal, which was opened in 1992, was upgraded as the Delegation of the European Commission to Nepal in 2002. Since 1996, donors and NGOs in Nepal faced increasing challenges of how to position themselves with respect to formal state (Royal) permission for internal access and for operating in rural areas increasingly governed by *de facto* Maoist authorities. After the breakdown of a ceasefire between the Maoists and Government of Nepal in August 2003, the European Commission, together with other bilateral donor agencies, adopted a set of "Basic Operating Guidelines" to emphasise the importance and responsibility of all parties to the conflict to maintain development space and provide access to beneficiaries in Nepal. These Guidelines relied considerably on internationally recognised principles of humanitarian law and reflect the specific conflict situation in the country.

The Basic Operating Guidelines were intended as operational guidelines or aspirations for development and humanitarian activities and for project partners and their staff to operate in Nepal. They were drafted and made public to indicate how donors operate in Nepal and to appeal to the parties in the conflict not to interfere in project activities. Similarly, in 2002 the United Kingdom's Department for International Development (DFID) and the German Federal Enterprise for International Cooperation (GiZ) in order to ensure that their programmes could continue safely and effectively without adversely affecting the ongoing conflict in Nepal, jointly established a Risk Management Office (RMO) based on the principle of "Risk Management" and "Do No Harm".[13]

The European Commission allocated €70 million as aid to Nepal in the *EU Country Strategy Paper (2002-2006)*.[14] In response to the Royal takeover, the Union suspended all programming activities in 2005 and the launch of new projects was put on hold due to the dissatisfaction with unfolding political events in Nepal. However, in that same year an ad-hoc commitment of €5 million was made outside the framework of the *Country Strategy Paper* for support to the Office of the High Commission on Human Rights (OHCHR) for strengthening monitoring of human rights. In addition, an ad hoc commitment of €7 million was made as a token of immediate support to the people's movement and Nepal's return to democracy. Norway and two EU Member States (Denmark and Finland) played an important role on influencing the EC decision during the Royal coup. All cooperation activities were reactivated in June 2006, thereby marking the EC's support for the democratisation process.

The EU's Conflict Resolution and Democratisation Agenda since 2006

After the April Revolution of 2006, the political coalition changed. The 250-year old Monarchy lost its prominence and the Maoists (once declared as terrorists), who had been undertaking a 10 year-old violent insurgency joined mainstream politics. This led to growing concerns among donors about engagement in Nepal and the intended or unintended impact of development or governance assistance on the very dynamics of the conflict. Most international development actors operating in Nepal had conducted their own conflict analyses, which came to the broad conclusion that economic deprivation and inequality were likely to indirectly impact the conflict and that further efforts to promote development were warranted both to ameliorate the effects of the conflict and tackle the underlying causes. There was, however, recognition that providing development assistance in itself does not necessarily contribute towards a peaceful resolution of the conflict and that any efforts had to be assessed on their individual merits.

Table 1: European Commission Country Strategy Paper, 2007–2013 (in million Euros)

Sector of Concentration	Amount	% of MIP
MIP I (2007-10)	**60**	**100**
Priority 1: Support to Education	36	60
Priority 2: Stability and Peace Building	22	36.5
Priority 3: Trade and Economic Capacity Building	2	3.4
MIP II (2011-13)	**60**	**100**
Priority 1: Support to Education	30-36	50-60
Priority 2: Stability and Peace Building	15-21	25-35
Priority 3: Trade and Economic Capacity Building	3-9	5-15
Total CSP	**120**	

Source: European Commission, *Nepal: Country Strategy Paper 2007-2013 – Mid-term Review Document IP 2011-2013* (Brussels: European Commission), 11 April 2010.

The April Revolution was followed by negotiations and the Comprehensive Peace Agreement, the establishment of the Interim Government and preparations for elections for the Constituent Assembly. Subsequently, different groups started to voice their dissatisfaction with the current state of affairs. Some of them took up arms in order to ensure that their voices were heard and that equal and proportional representation is ensured in the future political process. The issues of inclusion, participation and representation have become major, often heated, topics of discussion. The extent to which structures will be changed to include a wider segment of the society will be a determining factor for the success of the peace process. In this respect, many are looking at the contributions of the international community and the extent to which it can contribute to the ongoing peace process.

In the light of these rapid changes that were taking place in Nepal, Norway as well as EU Member States focused on the following three sectors in the *Country Strategy Paper (2007-2013)*:

education (with human rights, gender, conflict prevention and the environment as cross-cutting issues); stability and peace-building; and trade facilitation and promotion of trade and economic activities with an estimated budget of €120 million. The new *Strategy Paper* envisaged funding from 2007-2013 with a mid-term review held in 2010.

Impact of Conflict Resolution Initiatives of the European Union on Nepal

Minimum Engagement with Civil Society Organisations

The increased reliance of the European Union on budget support measures has delegated spending negotiations to individual donors and governments. As a result, civil society organisations (CSOs) have no significant role in affecting spending decisions. For example, there was no formal consultation process for CSOs in Nepal regarding *Country Strategy Paper* for 2007-2013. Moreover, the EC Delegation to Nepal is a sub-office of the larger EC Delegation to India, based in Delhi. Initiatives to consult with civil society more broadly are sometimes not possible, and it remains difficult to reach every NGO operating in the country.

The first installment of the Stability and Peace-building Grant of approximately €22 million under the *Country Strategy Paper (2007-2013)* was utilised mainly on three major sectors that constrained the civil society's resources for conflict resolution initiatives. Firstly, major EC grants were utilised for the Nepal Peace Trust Fund, which is a mechanism of the Government of Nepal for development partners as the preferred instrument for channelling support for the peace process. Secondly, major grants were provided for the observation of the Constituent Assembly Election of 2008. The European Commission provided funding for setting up national and international observation missions for monitoring elections. Brussels constituted an EU Election Observation Mission in 2008. The third category included major grants for strengthening government institutions such as the judiciary, training of government employees, peace and security training to security personnel like the Nepal Police and the Armed Police Force.

There are some components of Commission grants, which are disbursed directly to NGOs in Nepal, e.g. the European Initiative for Democracy and Human Rights (EIDHR), which has funded community-based organisations. However, major budgetary allocations have been made to specific targeted programmes of the government with limited funding for initiatives of civil society for conflict resolution.

A major challenge in EU's aid is "the 'de-concentration' of aid management from Brussels to the Commission Delegations (that) has rendered more serious the understaffing of local offices".[15] In fact, "With resources overstretched and often with limited political backing by the headquarters, Delegations tend to fall into a 'business as usual' approach, privileging infrastructure projects and their traditional role as aid managers rather than the more difficult and long-term conflict mitigation engagements".[16] Thus, this tends to give the impression that EU's funding for conflict resolution tends to prioritise big governmental programmes rather than focusing on small-scale grassroots conflict resolution or peace-building activities.

Ethnicisation of Issues

Ethnic issues have overshadowed political and economic issues during the country's political transition mainly because they have been well-funded from external donors to redress discrimination against marginalised communities. During 2010-2013, the Canadian International Development Agency (CIDA) had doled out Rs120 million to 19 ethnic groups and networks. The United Nations Development Programme has spent Rs25 million on 15 ethnic and regional networks to advocate for ethnic issues under a project on inclusive constitution. Since 2009, the Swiss Agency for Development Cooperation has been providing an annual budget of Rs 2.25 billion to the Constituent Assembly, political parties as well as other NGOs. The Danish HUGOU launched a project worth Rs

624 million called the Madhes Initiative. Similarly, the German aid agency (GiZ) has already spent Rs82.5 million during the first phase and an additional Rs110 million has been dispersed for discussion on federal issues. There are 34 EU projects supporting the ethnic agenda. The Union has been openly advocating ethnic issues in Nepal since 1998.

The European Instrument for Democracy and Human Rights is one of the major European initiatives for democracy building and human rights. The rights of the indigenous people are one of the major priorities under EIDHR. They seek to increase indigenous peoples' rights and capacity to control their own social, economic and cultural development, while enhancing territorial rights and capacity for sustainable management of biological resources. In a small country like Nepal with 103 recognised ethnic groups and a country, which is in transition to democracy, such over-emphasis of rights by the donor community is prolonging and adding major hurdles, especially as Nepal is now engaged in an experiment on demarking a federal set-up. Thus, a growing sense of ethno-nationalism is hampering the entire constitution-making process and prolonging the dilemma. The ethnic movement is now one of the major hurdles to peace and stability of Nepal.

Missionaries of some European countries like Finland, Denmark and Norway have been criticised for preaching Christianity in Nepal by "proselytizing poor Nepalese by offering material incentives".[17] Similarly, the European Union has been blamed by Hindu extremists for secularising Nepal, which used to be Hindu country till 2006. However, in the wake of the April Revolution and subsequent political developments, politicians decided to declare Nepal as a secular state. The European Union is often blamed for funding this "secularization"[18] campaign.

Centre–Periphery Disparity

In most developing countries, there are major socio-economic and cultural differences between the centre and the periphery. Nepal is no exception; there is a big difference between the environment in Kathmandu and the one outside the Valley. The international community was criticised for not being able to overcome the barriers and actually reach outside the capital. This, according to some, gives rise to discrepancies in information and that the international community's understanding of the national overview and complexities could be improved for better engagement.

Many EU projects seek to benefit people located outside the Kathmandu Valley. However, in practice a disproportionate amount of the funds for these projects are provided to NGOs and International Non-Governmental Organisations (INGOs) based in Kathmandu and a considerable amount of money is spent even before it reaches the intended project sites or the intended beneficiaries. Such projects tend to be designed and are implemented by the dominant groups, which are also recruited to implement through their own agencies. As a result, money is not spent in a way that would benefit the marginalised communities the most.

Similarly, the European Union's bureaucracy and complex process of funding proposals and onerous reporting mechanisms, make it virtually impossible for the local community-based organisation to access its funding. This creates disparity as only NGOs run by English-speaking elites have access to such funding. Some European donors have recently begun to channel funds to consultants and contractors, viz. the Department for International Development. In 2012, the DFID was blamed of channelling £500 million[19] to consultants and contractors. In fact, Nepal was one of the countries where more than 40 per cent of the aid budget was channelled to consultants and contractors in the name of aid effectiveness.

Divorce of Policy and Aid Harmonisation with European Partners

One of the major challenges for the European Union is the serious lack of coordination with its Member States, especially Germany, Finland, Denmark and the United Kingdom. Each of these countries is a very active partner of the conflict resolution process in Nepal. The United Kingdom with its DFID funds substantial grants which primarily are focused on Security Sector Reforms (SSR). Similarly, both Denmark and Finland are also primarily funding SSR programmes. Germany through the German Federal Enterprise for International Cooperation and other INGOs are working on rehabilitation of ex-Maoist combatants. Thus, making aid more effective by enhancing coordination and harmonisation between donors, ensuring alignment with partner countries' strategies and preparing the ground for more complementarity and division of labour by adopting multi-donor arrangements, such as co-financing or delegated cooperation is a must for aid harmonisation.

There are also many instances where there are policy indifferences between the European Union and its Member States. One popular instance that can be referred to is "the controversial sale" of more than 5,500 machine guns to Nepal by the Belgian Government in 2002, which were meant for the Government to fight the Maoist rebels. This had a serious impact on the posture of European Union, which was stressing the human rights accountability of the then Nepal Army. This deal also violated the EU Code of Conduct on Arms Exports which was adopted by the Cardiff European Council in June 1998 which stated: "Member States will not allow exports which would provoke or prolong armed conflicts or aggravate existing tensions or conflicts in the country of final destination."[20] Such indifference in policy can undermine the credibility of the European Union.

Conclusions: Treading on Water or Drowning?

In general the conflict resolution policies of the European Union are not based on a deep or common understanding of the reasons behind the conflicts or the forces that continue to separate the conflicting parties. The Union's policy has been reactive and driven by events rather than by long-term considerations. As such, it has not significantly contributed to conflict resolution. For instance, the EU's constant support to ethnic issues in Nepal is not resolving the conflict; on the contrary, it is creating bases for future conflicts ahead. Given the difficulties and varying complexity of conflicts, is the EU a viable actor in conflict resolution, or is it out of its depth? It has the potential to coordinate conflict resolution process among multitude donors of Nepal. However, Brussels has shied away from this role and preferred to involve itself in its own petty initiatives. Its policies have contributed to conflict resolution in a general way, but have not had a significant and measurable impact.

Conflict resolution initiatives of the EU in Nepal suffer as a result of the hesitation of Member States over adopting a harmonised aid policy, thereby creating a lot of duplicity and policy contrast. The European Union's focus on mainly funding government initiatives and less engagement with civil society organisations also constrains its capacity to make a difference in people's lives. Brussels' focus on Kathmandu-based NGOs is creating disparities amongst NGOs. This indicates that the Union continues to encounter problems of internal coherence even as it expands its profile and role in external relations. The EU faces some difficulties in extending the scope of its external relations activities. It has adopted some of the language of conflict resolution without developing the necessary tools and expertise that it needs to carry out the task. A more pragmatic, coordinated and robust approach towards conflicts and the conflicting parties could make all the difference between sustainable peace and the renewal of hostilities.

Notes

1. Micheal Merlingen and Rasa Ostraukaite, *European Union: Peacebuilding and Policing* (London: Routledge, 2006).
2. European Commission, *Nepal: Country Strategy Paper 2007-2013* (Brussels: European Commission, 2006).
3. European Commission, *Communication from the Commission on Conflict Prevention*, 11 April 2001.
4. John Burton, ed., *Conflict: Human Needs Theory* (London: Macmillan, 1990).
5. Vincent Kronenberger and Jan Wouters, eds., *The European Union and Conflict Prevention: Policy and Legal Aspects* (The Hague: Asser Press, 2005).
6. Johan Galtung, *Human Rights in Another Key* (Cambridge: Polity Press, 1994).
7. Oliver Richmond, *The Transformation of Peace* (London: Palgrave Macmillan, 2005).

8. European Commission, *Communication from the Commission on Conflict Prevention*, n. 3, pp. 8-9.
9. European Commission Conflict Prevention and Crisis Management Unit, *Report of the EC Conflict Prevention Assessment Mission* (Brussels: European Commission, 2002).
10. Stine Heiselberg, Sangeeta Lama, Judith Large, Guy Banim and Riika Marjamaki, *An Inclusive Peace Process in Nepal and Role of the EU, December 2007* (Helsinki: Crisis Management Initiative, 2007), p. 7.
11. Ibid., p. 7.
12. Ibid.
13. asud Hossain, Lauri Siitonen and Sudhindra Sharma, *Development Cooperation for Conflict Prevention and Conflict Resolution: Scope and Potentialities of Findland's Development Cooperation in Nepal* (Helsinki: Institute of Development Studies), University of Helsinki, Policy Paper 1/2006, p. 82.
14. European Commission, *Country Strategy Paper, Nepal and the European Community Cooperation Strategy 2002-2006*, 11 April 2001.
15. Fernanda Faria and Richard Youngs, *European Conflict Resolution Policies: Truncated Peacebuilding*, (Madrid: FRIDE, March 2012), p. 5.
16. Ibid., p. 5.
17. Jan Sharma, "Nepal's Faltering Peace Process: Civil Society, Media and International Community," in Ananda P. Shresta and Hari Uprety, eds., *Peacebuilding Process in Nepal* (Kathmandu: Nepal Foundation for Advanced Studies, 2008).
18. During the April Revolution (2006), a secular agenda was never a mainstream demand. However, much to the dismay of the Nepalese people, Nepal was declared a secular state in the first sitting of the re-instated House of Parliament on 18 May 2006. There is a deep suspicion among the Nepalese people that the secular agenda was exploited by European countries and received specific funding from Danish Church Aid and Finnish Church Aid.
19. Andrew Gilligan, "Poverty Barons' who Make a Fortune from Taxpayer-Funded Aid Budget," *The Telegraph*, 15 September 2012 (online), at URL:http://www.telegraph.co.uk/news/politics/9545584/Poverty-barons-who-make-a-fortune-from-taxpayer-funded-aid-budget.html (accessed on 15 February 2012).
20. Kyrre Holm, "Europeanising Export Controls: The Impact of the European Union Code of Conduct on Arms Exports in Belgium, Germany and Italy," *European Security*, 15(2), June 2006, pp. 213-234.

6
The European Union and Conflict Resolution in Sri Lanka

Rajendra K. Jain

Conflict resolution has been an overriding concern in almost all particular contexts that European diplomacy has engaged. Since the late 1990s, the European Union's conflict resolution activities have encompassed short-, medium- as well as long-term efforts which range from civilian and military crisis management, conflict settlement to state-building, democratisation and societal reconciliation. These actions seek to foster sustainable structural change in third countries, which, in turn, will induce conflict prevention, resolution and transformation.[1] Beyond its own borders, the Union has felt that it can contribute to conflict prevention by promoting political liberalisation, by making economic assistance conditional upon democratic reform, fostering development of civil society and non-governmental organisations and insistence on the protection of human rights.[2]

This chapter examines the European Union's approach towards the conflict in Sri Lanka. It evaluates its role of the Union as a Co-Chair of the Sri Lanka Donor Group, the impact of the ban on the Liberation Tigers of Tamil Eelam (LTTE), termination of GSP Plus and reaction of Brussels towards human rights violations in Sri Lanka. In conclusion, the chapter discusses Indian perceptions of the EU's role in conflict resolution in Sri Lanka and evaluates the causes of failure of external engagement.

EU Approach towards the Conflict in Sri Lanka

Being a small middle-income country, far from Europe without substantial economic stakes or strategic resources, Sri Lanka has generally received only limited attention from the international community. Europe paid scant attention to the conflict in Sri Lanka, particularly when compared to its involvement in the conflicts in the Balkans or the Middle East. The European Union generally felt that it had "no vested interest in Sri Lanka; that it could contribute positively to the peace process".[3] However, few in Europe "know where Sri Lanka is. Few states are concerned. Every time there is a discussion about policy and strategy, there is never a problem in reaching a consensus".[4]

After the conflict broke out between the LTTE and the Sri Lankan Government in July 1983, the key focus of the European Community's development aid was relief and rehabilitation, which played a major role in alleviating the plight of the displaced persons in the conflict areas of the country.[5] However, EC aid was "quite compartmentalized" with ECHO funding relief and rehabilitation in the North and East and traditional development cooperation and, more recently, economic cooperation in the South. This approach had been criticised by some observers for increasing regional imbalances and feeding the conflict.[6] Many EU Member States were keen to see a resolution to the conflict because of the spillover effect in terms of Sri Lankan asylum-seekers in the EU.[7] A vocal Tamil diaspora was another factor driving donor agencies' attention to the conflict.

Until the 2000s, Sri Lanka was much more the subject of development policy than its political foreign policy. The limited interest in Sri Lanka was also evident from the fact that until 2005, the EC Delegation in Colombo had a solitary diplomat and supporting staff. Partly because of the small size of the Delegation and partly because all aid was dispersed indirectly, through partners, the EU and Sri Lanka were "virtually invisible to each other".[8]

The EU and Norway as Peace Facilitator

The European Union regarded Norway's role as a peace mediator in Sri Lanka since 1999 as "well established and has proven to be a most valuable asset".[9] In February 2002, a ceasefire agreement between the Government of Sri Lanka and the LTTE under Norwegian auspices seemed to offer prospects of ending violence. Post-9/11, the global war on terror and the banning of the LTTE by the United States (1997), Canada and the United Kingdom (2001) and Australia, there was growing pressure to enter into peaceful negotiations. This was coupled by pressure by the Tamil diaspora to accept the ceasefire and commence negotiations. To oversee the ceasefire and monitor compliance, the Sri Lankan Monitoring Mission (SLMM)[10] comprising of monitors from the Nordic countries (Norway, Sweden, Denmark, Finland and Iceland) was established to investigate alleged violations. Despite problems bedevilling the peace process, the ceasfire between the Government of Sri Lanka and the LTTE held for nearly four years. In early 2006, the ceasefire collapsed with a series of ambushes of government soldiers by the LTTE, which led to retaliatory measures by the Sri Lankan Government.

Since the ceasefire agreement (February 2002), the European Union, like other donors, sought to encourage the Sri Lankan government and the LTTE to work together towards a political solution based on power-sharing and federalism. Donors hoped that peace would create more opportunities for investment and development assistance to Sri Lanka, leading to "a substantial peace dividend".[11] EU's active engagement in the Sri Lankan peace process was governed by the following objectives:

- providing support for the search for a peaceful negotiated solution to the conflict and in case of a peace settlement, engage in the rehabilitation and reconstruction activities in the North and East to provide a sustainable basis for a lasting peace;
- providing support to measures and actions aimed at improving democracy, good governance and human rights and eventually community reconciliation activities through the various available budget lines;
- providing humanitarian assistance and food security to the conflict areas in order to alleviate the effects of the conflict.[12]

EU as Co-Chair

Norway and the three other Co-Chairs—the United States, the European Union and Japan—of the Sri Lanka Donor Group (SLDG) organised two major international donor conferences in Oslo (November 2002) and Tokyo (June 2003) as well as a preparatory meeting in Washington. As the Co-Chairs, they contributed to the peace process in three major ways: by facilitating the political negotiations, in reconstruction and rehabilitation and by moderating the LTTE's behaviour. The EU stance was "most closely aligned" with that of Norway as they both endorsed the disbursement of development assistance towards the reconstruction of the northern and eastern parts of Sri Lanka.[13] The Co-Chairs comprised a kind of "*ad hoc* group of international players that had assumed a degree of ownership of the conflict in Sri Lanka".[14] However, the Union was apparently a "reluctant" Co-Chair which was roped in as a result of Sri Lankan diplomatic efforts.[15]

At the Tokyo Donor Conference (June 2003), pledges totalled US$4.5 billion for relief and rehabilitation work in the conflict-affected north-eastern region. However, this assistance was contingent on the continuation of the peace process and its monitoring by the international community. The "peace conditionalities" included progress on human rights, democracy, federalism and the rule of law, which were linked to structural issues. Other conditions stressed allowing Muslim participation in peace talks and establishing effective delivery channels for fostering development activities in north-eastern Sri Lanka.

The Union committed $293 million over a three-year period at the Tokyo conference. Out of this, the EU agreed to contribute €50 million for 2003-2004 which included its earlier commitment of €17.5 million at the Sri Lanka Peace Process Support meeting held in Oslo in November 2002. Brussels clarified that a part of the agreed development aid was conditional on the resumption of the peace process, particularly €5.3 million allotted for the North East Reconstruction Fund allotted for 2003.[16] However, with the exclusion of the LTTE from the Tokyo conference, the momentum of the peace process began to wane. This, in turn, crippled the donors' initiative and the assistance promised remained on paper. The lack of progress in the peace talks was also attributed to a paucity of strong consensus amongst donors regarding the process and on any form of aid conditionality. Some EU Member States were arguably "uneasy with the US dominance in influencing the course of the peace process". Even Europeans could not see eye-to-eye on certain issues such as the areas of development or the work to be done in these areas. Some also perceived Norway to be sympathetic towards the LTTE and did not prefer its role as the facilitator of the peace process while others backed the Sri Lankan Government.[17]

At a meeting with EU counterparts in Brussels on 8 December 2003, Assistant Secretary of State for South Asia Christina Rocca urged the Union not to treat the LTTE as co-equal with the Government of Sri Lanka. The EU interlocuters "listened politely", but avoided a discussion that would force them to defend External Affairs Commissioner Chris Patten's recent visit on 26 November 2003 to meet LTTE commander Velupillai Prabhakaran at the outfit's northern headquarters.[18]

The Co-Chairs met periodically in various fora and issued strong statements in a bid to sustain the peace process and get the parties to return to the negotiating table.[19] In the run-up to the April 2004 polls, the Co-Chairs urged all political figures to work to ensure a free, fair and peaceful election, while calling for the "campaign rhetoric" to be "devoid of religious and ethnic intolerance". They were also anxious that "important gains. . . made in the peace process" were not undermined.[20]

At a Co-Chair meeting in Colombo on 25 October 2005, the Co-Chairs had concluded that the assumptions underlying the so-called "Tokyo Process", viz. that "both sides were serious about a negotiated settlement within the framework of a united Sri Lanka (b) that both sides, especially the LTTE, would respond to economic incentives to continue the peace process and (c) that the Tigers would change from a military organisation into a political one—have not been realised".[21]

The Co-Chairs had been formed in a different environment with the specific task of ensuring compliance of the LTTE and the Government of Sri Lanka with the "Tokyo Declaration". However, with the end of the ceasefire and the resumption of hostilities, their initial *raison d'etre* no longer existed. However, EU Ambassador to Sri Lanka, Julian Wilson, still maintained that the Co-Chairs still had a valuable role to play in supporting Norway's role as facilitator and keeping the spotlight on Sri Lanka. It was also realised that the effectiveness of economic assistance as an incentive to either party had been exaggerated.[22]

EU bans the LTTE, May 2006

Western liberal democracies, generally speaking, tended to tolerate the presence and activity of foreign insurgent and terrorist groups unless these activities adversely affected domestic security and foreign policy interests. The high degree of tolerance and self-interest of host countries had facilitated the growth of formidable international support structures for terrorist and insurgent groups like the LTTE.[23] On 19 May 2000, the European Parliament adopted a resolution urging Member States to initiate steps to proscribe the LTTE in order to prevent it from raising any financial resources to further its war in Sri Lanka.

Perceptions of the LTTE had changed somewhat following the 9/11 attacks, but it still did not figure in the list of 12 organisations banned by the EU in December 2001. Some observers attributed this to effective LTTE lobbying of parliamentarians of continental Europe.[24] Among European countries, the United Kingdom took the initiative in 2001 in banning the LTTE and freezing its assets largely because it had the largest Tamil diaspora in Europe.[25] The EU was extremely critical of the assassination of Foreign Minister Lakshman Kadirgamar (12 August 2005), which reflected the clear intention of the killers to "restart conflict".[26] "The pursuit of political goals with its totally unacceptable methods only serves to damage the LTTE standing and credibility as a negotiating partner," said the EU.[27]

On 26 September 2005, the European Union barred the Tamil Tigers from visiting its 25 Member States and declared that it was "actively considering the formal listing of the LTTE as a terrorist organisation".[28] The announcement generated an intensive internal debate in the Union with many within the Union resisting the step. Six months later, when Washington pressed the EU on listing the LTTE as a terrorist organisation, Brussels could only respond that consultations among EU Member States on this issue would "take time" since no consensus had yet been forged.[29] Some argued that a high level of proof was needed. France and Italy had objected to the listing on procedural grounds because they felt that they were being pushed into it by the United States. The Nordic EU Member States (Denmark, Sweden and Finland) had objected out of solidarity with Norway and its negotiating role and due to their own activities in the region. They also urged that a listing be accompanied by a statement outlining the failings of both the Government and the LTTE. Commissioner Ferrero-Waldner and her colleague Herve Jouanjean, Deputy Director-General for External Relations in charge of Asia and Latin America, had pushed for "a lesser sanction than listing—some type of targeted sanctions—but had lost".[30]

The proscription of the LTTE was expected to severely hamper its efforts to raise funding to finance its clandestine arms procurement programme. But it also had "a political cost" in that it could jeopardise the brittle CFA and lead to a full retraction of the LTTE from the peace process.[31] Some political groups in the European Parliament considered it a mistake and that the EU had taken sides by banning the LTTE.[32] The ban was tantamount to an overall *volte face* of external actors which had previously viewed the Tamil Tigers more leniently, but it did hinder access to its fund-raising activities from the Tamil diaspora in Europe. However, it failed to deter the LTTE from resorting to military means.

After the imposition of the ban on the LTTE on 30 May 2006,[33] the LTTE argued that the EU was no longer "an honest broker" and informed Brussels to withdraw EU Member State (Sweden, Finland and Denmark) monitors[34] of the Norwegian-led Sri Lanka

Monitoring Mission (SLMM), established to oversee compliance of the ceasefire agreement in three months.[35] Thereafter, it became difficult for the EU to maintain influence on the ground. As Amaia Sanchez-Cacicedo rightly points out,

> The EU ban epitomises how the liberal internationalist regime flexed its muscle through a regional organisation to punish a separatist rebel group for breaching global governance norms within the parameters of a liberal peace. . . . The ban on the Tigers not only signalled a move towards normative appropriateness, but also towards putting an end to what was acknowledged as the Tamil Tigers' instrumentalisation of the peace process. This policy shift by the EU became growingly aligned with US policy towards Sri Lanka in the later stages of the peace process.[36]

The Collapse of the Ceasefire

Since the collapse of the ceasefire, the European Union's role in resolving the Sri Lankan conflict was highlighted in the *Country Strategy Paper for Sri Lanka (2007-2013)*. The principles that guided the EU's policy towards Sri Lanka were based on the fungibility of aid (aid that may benefit the government but should not pass through the budget), conflict sensitivity (ensuring aid projects are designed to be feasible in conflict and if possible, alleviate conflict conditions) and peace dividend (ensuring aid acts as an incentive for conflict resolution and prevention).[37] The EU's development policy towards Sri Lanka also emphasised conflict prevention and conflict resolution. It sought to make its response strategy conflict-sensitive and was to strengthen Sri Lankan efforts to find a political solution to the conflict and address the development challenges in the north and east of the country. By treating Sri Lanka as a "conflict country in crisis", its aim was to ensure flexibility of implementation to meet demands on the ground and to maintain the efficiency and the effectiveness of its aid to the country.[38] "Peace negotiations within the CFA framework did take place in Geneva during 2006 and the like-minded donors continued to provide financial assistance, despite the rising violence.

Western countries and International Financial Institutions (IFIs) disbursed substantial foreign aid to Sri Lanka in 2006 and 2007, though Japan was the leading bilateral donor and China was quickly catching up."[39] From 2007 onwards, Asian donors, especially China and Japan, led the list of bilateral donors. The Co-Chairs went from "monitoring the implementation of the peace process and funding reconstruction activities to crisis diplomacy, which had not been part of their original liberal peace strategy".[40]

Termination of GSP Plus

In the aftermath of the 2004 tsunami, the European Union granted Sri Lanka GSP Plus trade benefits from 1 July 2005 which led to a substantial increase in Sri Lankan exports to the EU.[41] In the period 2007-2008, Brussels exerted considerable pressure on Sri Lanka to end military operations against the LTTE and threatened to terminate GSP Plus benefits. In October 2008, an "investigation" was launched into GOSL's implementation of the 27 international conventions on core human rights and conventions on environment and good governance principles. The European Commission recommended (19 October 2009) withdrawal of Sri Lanka's GSP-Plus benefits.[42] In June 2010, Colombo rejected a EU proposal that it commit to fulfill 15 conditions in order to enjoy further extension of the GSP Plus facility, as the conditions imposed by Brussels sought to erode the Government of Sri Lanka's authority to deal with sensitive domestic issues.[43] Subsequently, on 16 February 2010 Brussels decided to temporarily suspend GSP Plus from 15 August 2010 in view of "shortcomings" in respect of Sri Lanka's implementation of three United Nations human rights conventions, viz. the International Convention on Civil and Political Rights, the Convention against Torture, and the Convention on the Rights of the Child. The loss of GSP Plus trade benefits (estimated at €78 million in 2008) was relatively small and was not likely to have any major impact on the Sri Lankan economy or the Rajapaksa regime.[44] The EU considers the GSP Plus to be a "closed chapter".[45]

Human Rights Violations

The European Union had been consistently critical of human rights violations by the LTTE. In mid-August 2004, the Union condemned the political killings, child recruitment and abductions increasingly being committed as a breach of fundamental human rights. Brussels asserted that adhering to good governance, pluralism, human rights and democracy were vital if the rebels were to obtain "recognition as a political player" in Sri Lanka.[46] However, it was only with the end of the ceasefire in early 2006 that there was a general feeling of "fatigue, frustration and futility" amongst international donors, with several EU Member States, especially the UK and Germany, which reduced their assistance to Sri Lanka and their criticism of Sri Lanka, especially human rights, increased.[47] The European Union expressed its deep concern about the evolving humanitarian crisis and the vast number of Internally Displaced People (IDPs) trapped by the fighting in northern Sri Lanka as well as the continuing reports of high civilian casualties.[48]

After the LTTE's defeat in May 2009, which had brought the war to an end and cost over 100,000 lives apart from social, economic and military losses, the EU unsuccessfully tried to push for international action at the UN Security Council and the UN Human Rights Council. A visit to the field by EU *troika* representatives at Deputy Foreign Minister level in March 2009 was apparently "heavily stage-managed" by the Sri Lankan Government and "little real investigation" was allowed.[49] On 18 May 2009, the EU called for an independent inquiry into alleged human rights violations resulting from the conflict in Sri Lanka and demanded that those responsible to be held to account.

At a special session of the United Nations Human Rights Council (28 May 2009) to investigate the reported war crimes and atrocities committed by both the LTTE and the Sri Lankan armed forces, the Swiss–EU draft resolution calling for an investigation into possible war crimes was not adopted.[50] The Union continued to be concerned about the continuing humanitarian crisis and the "unacceptable" situation of an estimated quarter of a million internally displaced persons still detained in closed camps. It expressed willingness to support reconstruction and development in eastern and northern Sri Lanka under certain conditions (e.g. freedom of movement of returnees). It called for an end to all human rights violations and reiterated its call for possible violations of international humanitarian law by all actors to be subject to "independent and credible inquiry".[51]

Responding to calls for an inquiry into allegations of war crimes, the Sri Lankan Government set up a Lessons Learnt and Reconciliation Commission (LLRC) in May 2010. The European Union urged Sri Lanka to address the issue of accountability over alleged human rights abuses committed during the final stages of the conflict and to engage with UN Secretary General Ban Ki-moon on the contents of the 'Report of the UN Secretary General's Panel of Experts on Accountability in Sri Lanka' (12 April 2011) on the war in Sri Lanka, which had concluded that there are credible allegations of major violations of international human rights and humanitarian law committed by all sides in the conflict, during its final stages.[52]

In March 2012, the European Union voted for the US sponsored resolution asking Sri Lanka to fully implement the recommendations of the Lessons Learnt and Reconciliation Commission (LLRC) following the end of the war in 2009. Like the United States, the EU regarded the report to be incomplete. It noted that it had not adequately addressed allegations that war crimes had been committed during the final months of the civil war and called for steps to be taken to remedy its weakness.

On 10 December 2013, the EU asked Sri Lanka to allow free access to UN officials investigating the allegations of human rights violations. On 27 March 2014, the EU supported a US-sponsored resolution at the UN Human Rights Council requesting the Office of the High Commissioner for Human Rights to undertake a comprehensive investigation into alleged serious violations and abuses of human rights and related crimes by both parties in Sri Lanka during the period covered by the LLRC (21 February 2002 until 15 November 2011), when it presented its report to the President of Sri Lanka.

India and the EU Role

Indian approval of Norway, which brokered a ceasefire agreement in February 2002 between the LTTE and the Government of Sri Lanka, as an intermediary was greatly influenced by the "pronounced distaste" in India of great powers becoming more directly involved in South Asian internal affairs.[53] Brussels was keen that New Delhi play a larger role in helping to resolve the Sri Lankan crisis. Though regional peace and security has been discussed in the political and security dialogues, including the EU–India Security Dialogue, India has not encouraged repeated EU attempts to have the developments in Sri Lanka covered within the ambit of the EU–India Security Dialogue.[54] Inevitably the changes in India's strategic perception were reflected in its approach to Sri Lanka's war against the LTTE, particularly after the failure of the peace process 2002. Its role had been limited as "an advisor and counsellor" not only to Sri Lanka but to the four Co-Chairs—the European Union, Japan, Norway and the U.S. —which promoted the peace process.[55] The growing involvement of the international community in the peace process effectively curtailed India's strategic space in its sensitive neighbourhood.[56]

After the defeat of the LTTE in May 2009, India has been willing to work with the United States, the United Nations, the EU and others interested in the situation in Sri Lanka to address the humanitarian effort on an urgent basis. Domestic political compulsions (Dravida Munnetra Kazhagam—the political party in Tamil Nadu which was a coalition partner in the United Progressive Alliance) had been responsible for India voting against Sri Lanka in the UN Human Rights Council on several occasions. These constraints have been mitigated to a certain extent by the absolute majority secured by the Bharatiya Janata Party (BJP)-led National Democratic Alliance coalition under Prime Minister Narendra Modi in the parliamentary elections of May 2014.

Conclusion

During the Sri Lankan peace process (2002-2006), the European Union encouraged negotiations and applied some pressure on the LTTE by labelling it as a terrorist organisation and imposing sanctions, but it had little influence. Despite being Sri Lanka's biggest export market and its fourth largest donor, the European Union had little impact because of the greater regional influence of China and India and its failure to respond to political trends and opportunities in a timely manner in Sri Lanka. Another major reason was the lack of effective coordination amongst EU Member States[57] in coordinating freezing of development aid and continued arms sales to Sri Lanka.[58] The Union's influence was limited primarily due to the contrasting positions, the limited political will of its Member States, and the lack of effective coordination amongst Co-Chairs who often pulled in different directions.[59] Discrepancies among external actors made them appear weak in the eyes of domestic stakeholders. For instance, amongst the Co-Chairs while Norway and the Union favoured "appeasement" of the LTTE, the United States adopted a hard-line approach.[60]

The approach of the Co-Chairs was "to try and bribe the state to negotiate with the LTTE and reform the machinery of the state so that it protects minorities from majority excess".[61] However, the promise of increased funds to Sri Lanka and the threat of withholding these funds

> did not nothing to persuade either the LTTE or the Government of Sri Lanka to continue negotiations. This attempt to encourage the peacemaking process was not helped by the fact that the sum promised included previous commitments, and donors had no mechanism to withhold funds in the pipeline. Rather than sustain the peacemaking process, the prioritisation of economic recovery may have weakened it.[62]

EU interlocuters also acknowledged that the Sri Lankan Government was not sensitive to economic pressure.[63] The donors were unable to deliver the bulk of the aid to the conflict-affected areas of north-eastern Sri Lanka because of the extremely difficult situation on the ground. The external powers overestimated their "ability to 'correct' internal contradictions through the delivery of aid".[64] One of the inherent difficulties of the peace process was that "a democratically elected government with the legitimate use of force was being asked to negotiate with a proscribed terrorist organisation to decide how the existing structures, which serve the Government well, should be reformed".[65]

As violence increased, the EU, unlike Norway, became increasingly vocal about human rights violations by the parties, particularly the LTTE. The assassination of Foreign Minister Lakshman Kadirgamar, in August 2005 allegedly by the Tamil Tigers, triggered Europe's shift to a hard-line stance towards the LTTE.[66] Brussels had been concerned about a more authoritarian streak in President Rajapaksa after his re-election for a second term in January 2010: "The plane seems to be heading for Singapore, but it might land in Burma."[67]

In the later stages of the peace process, the Western Powers resorted to a 'responsibility to protect' discourse, which was more appropriate to a humanitarian intervention scenario than to conflict resolution.[68] The external actors "overestimated the influence of international material and normative structures on the parties. In doing so, they disregarded the relevance of regional and domestic structures".[69] The Co-Chairs were "able to reward but not to penalise" as there was no mechanism in place that allowed donors to reward the parties for progress and penalise them for failure.[70]

Like the United States, the European Union also adopted the method of 'naming and shaming' the LTTE whenever the group drifted from its commitment to the peace process or engaged in activities antithetical to the agreed norms and conditions of peace-making. However, neither the internationalisation of the peace process nor the various measures taken by the international community succeeded in creating a sense of urgency and seriousness in the LTTE for a negotiated peace settlement, but they did constitute a major factor to deter the resumption of war.[71]

The entire focus of the peace process was on Track I, i.e. between the LTTE and the Government of Sri Lanka. In fact, "little was done to reconcile the North and the South, the elite-level peace negotiations stalled before any of the contentious issues were raised, and the peace dividend failed to materialise".[72] External actors did not undertake a holistic view towards conflict resolution and paid inadequate attention to the challenges confronted at the Track 2 and 3 levels, which are critical to the achievement of sustainable peace.

Notes

1. Nathalie Tocci, "The EU in Conflict Resolution," in Wolff Stefan and Christalla Yakinthou, eds., *Conflict Resolution: Theories and Practice* (London, 2011), p. 4.
2. Cf. Susanne Baier-Allen, "Conflict Prevention through Development Cooperation: The EU Approach in the Maghreb," in Peter Cross and G. Rasamoelina, eds., *Conflict Prevention Policy of the European Union: Recent Engagements, Future Instruments* (Baden-Baden: Nomos, 1999), pp. 44-45.
3. Author Interview, Brussels, 10 December 2008.
4. Author Interview, Brussels, 10 December 2008.
5. European Union, Commission, *The EC and Sri Lanka Cooperation Strategy—The EC and Sri Lanka, 2002-2006*, pp. 17-18.
6. European Commission, Conflict Prevention and Crisis Management Unit, *EC Conflict Assessment Mission, Sri Lanka, August 2002*, Rienzie Perera, Morgan MacSwiney, pp. 38-39.
7. The number of Sri Lankan asylum-seekers in the industrialised countries had decreased steadily since 2000. In 2000, 16,380 persons from Sri Lanka applied for asylum in the 29 industrialised countries of the world. In 2001, the number was 14,441 and in 2002 it was 10,158. In 2002, Sri Lankans comprised the ninth largest group of asylum-seekers worldwide. Of the other 10,158 applications, 7,519 were submitted within the EU. Of these, nearly half were lodged in the UK. United Nations High Commissioner for Refugees, *Background Paper on Refugees and Asylum-Seekers from Sri Lanka*, 30 April 2004, p. 58, available at http://www.unhcr.org/refworld/docid/40d837/42.html (accessed 10 October 2012).
8. Marlies Glasius and Denisa Kostovicova, "The European Union as a State-Builder: Policies towards Serbia and Sri Lanka," in Julia Raue and Patrick Sutter, eds., *Facets and Practices of State-Building* (Leiden: Martinus Nijhoff, 2009), p. 142.
9. *EC Conflict Assessment Mission, Sri Lanka, August 2002*, n. 6, note 49.
10. The Sri Lanka Monitoring Mission (SLMM) was an autonomous international organisation, established by the two Parties to the Sri Lanka Ceasefire Agreement (CFA) of 2002, as an impartial instrument to monitor the agreement. The SLMM was set up as a civilian mission jointly financed and staffed by the five Nordic countries.
11. Adam Burke and Anthea Mulakala, "An Insider's View of Donor Support for the Sri Lankan Peace Process, 2000-2005," in Jonathan Goodhand, Jonathan Spencer and Benedikt Korf, eds., *Conflict and Peacebuilding in Sri Lanka: Caught in the Peace Trap?* (London: Routlege, 2011), p. 158.

12. *The EC and Sri Lanka Cooperation Strategy—The EC and Sri Lanka, 2002-2006*, n. 5, pp. 24-25.
13. Amaia Sanchez-Cacicedo, "Sri Lanka: What Role for the EU?", *ISS Opinion* (Paris: European Union Institute for Security Studies, 2009), p. 2.
14. Jon Oskar Solnes, *A Powderkeg in Paradise: Lost Opportunity for Peace in Sri Lanka* (New Delhi: Konark Publisers, 2010.), p. 389.
15. Ibid., p. 389; Keith Noyahr, "The Role of the International Community," in Kumar Rupesinghe, ed., *Negotiating Peace in Sri Lanka: Efforts, Failures and Lessons*, vol. 2 (Colombo: Foundation for Co-existence, 2006), p. 367.
16. "Tokyo Conference on Re-construction and Development of Sri Lanka", European Union @ United Nations, 6 June 2003, [Online web] (accessed on 29 April 2012). URL: http://www.eu-un.europa.eu/articles/en/article_2402_en.htm.
17. S.D. Muni, "Sri Lanka's Peace Process: Donors as Peace Makers," in V. R. Raghavan and Volker Bauer, eds., *Federalism and Conflict Resolution in Sri Lanka* (New Delhi: Lancer Publishers, 2006), p. 92.
18. Wikileaks, "A/S Rocca Consultations on South Asia with EU Commission," 11 December 2003, at http://wikileaks.org/cable/2003/12/03BRUSSELS5593.html.
19. Keith Noyahr, "The Role of the International Community," in Kumar Rupasinghe, ed., *Negotiating Peace in Sri Lanka: Efforts, Failures and Lessons* (Colombo: Foundation for Co-existence, 2006), vol. 1, p. 393.
20. Co-Chairs statement, 17 February 2004.
21. Wikileaks, "Sri Lanka: Co-Chairs Preview Possible Role Post-Election; Check Pulse on Peace Process," 27 October 2005, at http://wikileaks.org/cable/2005/10/05COLOMBO1859.html.
22. Ibid.
23. Rohan Gunaratna, "Sri Lanka: Feeding the Tamil Tigers," in Karen Ballentine and Jake Sherman, eds., *The Political Economy of Armed Conflict: Beyond Greed and Grievance* (Boulder, Col: Lynne Rienner, 2003), p. 215.
24. Ibid., p. 216.
25. In 1997, 250,000 Tamils lived in Europe: UK 90,000; France 60,000; Germany 50,000; Switzerland 35,000; Norway 20,000; Denmark 15,000; Sweden 5,000. Cited in Rohan Gunaratna, "Impact of the Mobilized Tamil Diaspora on the Protracted Conflict in Sri Lanka," in Kumar Rupesinghe, ed., *Negotiating Peace in Sri Lanka: Efforts, Failures and Lessons,* (Colombo: Foundation for Co-existence, 2006), vol. 1, 2nd edition, p. 288.
26. Statement by Commissioner Benito Ferrero-Waldner on the Kadirgamar killing, 13 August 2005.
27. EU Declaration, 26 September 2005.
28. European Declaration condemning Terrorism in Sri Lanka, 26 September 2005, at http://www.europa.eu.
29. Cable on the meeting of Assistant Secretary for State for South and Central Asia Richard A. Boucher with Sri Lanka Co-Chairs in Oslo, 28 March 2006. Wikileaks, "Sri Lanka Co-Chairs Meeting in Oslo," 11 May 2006.
30. Wikileaks, "Tokyo Co-Chairs Pre-Meetings," 25 May 2006 at aebr.home.x54all.nl/wl/aftenposten/srilanka.html; Shamindra Ferdinando, "Netherlands: Italy, France Felt US Behind Move, Opposed LTTE Proscription by EU," *The Island*

(Colombo), 23 January 2011; Lucia Kubosova, "EU Blacklist of Tamil Tigers May Harm Peace Talks," 29 May 2005, at euobserver.com/foreign/21706 (accessed on 8 August 2014).

31. Jon Oskar Solnes, *A Powderkeg in Paradise: Lost Opportunity for Peace in Sri Lanka* (New Delhi: Konark Publishers, 2010), p. 111.
32. Author Interview, Brussels, 23 November 2006.
33. Statement by the EU Presidency, 29 May 2006. See "Ban on LTTE No Surprise," *The Hindu*, 1 June 2006.
34. Norwegian Ministry of Foreign Affairs, *Replacement of SLMM Monitors from EU countries*, Press Release, 22 June 2006, [Online web] (accessed on 2 May 2012), URL: http://www.regjeringen.no/nb/dep/ud/pressesenter/pressemeldinger/2006/Replacement-of-SLMM-monitors-from-EU-countries.html?id=419966.
35. The Tamil Tigers would not accept 39 EU nationals from Nordic EU Member States as monitors after 1 September 2006 because the Union had proscribed them as a terrorist organisation. However, the remaining 18 monitors from non-EU Member States (Norway and Iceland) would remain to monitor the crumbling ceasefire. The operation of SLMM ceased in January 2008.
36. Amaia Sanchez-Cacicedo, *Building States, Building Peace: Global and Regional Involvement in Sri Lanka and Myanmar* (Basingstoke: Palgrave Macmillan, 2014), p. 140.
37. European Union, Commission, *Country Strategy Paper for Sri Lanka 2007-2013*, p. 20.
38. Ibid.
39. Sanchez-Cacicedo, n. 36, p. 141.
40. Ibid.
41. Sri Lankan exports to the EU increased from €1.6 billion in 2005 to roughly €2.2 billion in 2008. Apparel exports during the same period increased from €827 million to €1.2 billion.
42. See http://trade.ec.europa.eu/doclib/docs/2009 /october/tradedoc 145152.pdf.
43. http://www.srilankaembassy.be/EU.htm (accessed 23 February 2013).
44. Clare Castillejo, "Sri Lanka: The Failure of EU Human Rights Sanctions," *FRIDE Policy Brief*, no. 63, January 2011, p. 2.
45. EU Ambassador to Sri Lanka, Bernard Savage, remarked: "The fact is GSP+ was withdrawn and Sri Lanka has not reapplied. We need to move on." Cited in Feizal Samath, "Rights Issues Mar Sri Lanka-EU Trade," International Press Service News Agency, 19 August 2012, at http://www.ipsnews.net/2012/08/rights-issues-mar-sri-lanka-eu-trade/.
46. See V.S. Sambandan, "E.U. Concerned at 'Human Rights Violations' by the LTTE," *The Hindu*, 17 August 2004.
47. Adam Burke and Anthea Mulakala, "An Insider's View of Donor Support for the Sri Lankan Peace Process, 2000-2005," in Jonathan Goodhand, Jonathan Spencer and Benedikt Korf, eds., *Conflict and Peacebuilding in Sri Lanka: Caught in the Peace Trap?* (London: Routlege, 2011), p. 164.
48. Council of the European Union, Conclusions on Sri Lanka, 2925th General Affairs Council meeting, 23 February 2009.
49. Remarks by ECHO Head of Unit Esko Kentrschynskyj in Wikileaks, "U.S.-EU

Consultations on Humanitarian Assistance," 3 June 2009, at http://wikileaks.org/cable/2009/06/09BRUSSELS769.html.

50. See EU Press Statement, "Human Rights Council Special Session on Sri Lanka," Geneva, 28 May 2009, Council of the European Union, Press Release 10472/09 (Presse 158).
51. Council of the European Union, Council Conclusions on Sri Lanka, 2971st External Relations Council Meeting, Luxembourg, 27 October 2009.
52. Easwaran Rutnam, "EU To Press Sri Lanka," *The Sunday Leader* (Colombo), 8 September 2011.
53. Alan Bullion, "Norway and the Peace Process in Sri Lanka," *Civil Wars*, 4(3), Autumn 2001, pp. 79-92.
54. B. Raman, "India and China in Europe," 11 October 2010 at http://www.southasiaanalysis.org/%5Cpapers41%5Cpaper4089.html, accessed 7 January 2012.
55. Col. R Hariharan, "Revisiting India's Sri Lanka Policy Options," 14 August 2009, at http://www.colhariharan.org/2009/08/revisiting-indias-sri-lanka-policy.html.
56. S.D. Muni, "Peace without Process: Sri Lanka's Dilemma," in B. Raman, N. Sathiya Moorthy and Kalpana Chittaranjan, eds., *Sri Lanka, Peace without a Process* (New Delhi: Samskriti, 2006), p. xxxiv.
57. Castillejo, n. 44, p. 1 and 4.
58. Many EU Member States (including Bulgaria, the Czech Republic, Slovakia, the UK, France, Italy, the Netherlands and Poland) continued to arm the Sri Lankan Government since the election of President Mahinda Rajapaksa in 2005. For instance, in 2007 nine EU Member States authorised arms sales to Sri Lanka valued at €4.09 million. The licensed material ranged from small weapons, ammunition and explosives to missiles, ground vehicles, naval vessels and aircraft. East European Member States mainly supplied small arms while Western Member States sold bigger hardware. In 2008, Slovakia authorised the sale of 10,000 rockets to Colombo. See Leigh Philipps, "While Condemning Sri Lanka Violence, EU Still Sells Arms to Government," 19 May 2009, at euobserver.com/defence/28155. Britain approved commercial sales of more than £13.6 million, including armoured vehicles, machine gun components and semi-automatic pistols. Sarah Holt, Aid, *Peacebuilding and the Resurgence of War: Buying Time in Sri Lanka* (Basingstoke: Palgrave Macmillan, 2011), p. 104.
59. P. Sahadevan, "The Peace Process: Role of the International Community," in A. Bansal, M. Mayilvaganan and S. Podder, eds., *Sri Lanka: Search for Peace* (New Delhi: Manas Publications, 2007), p. 113; Castillejo, n. 44, pp. 1, 3-4.
60. Sanchez-Cacicedo, n. 36, p. 149.
61. Holt, n. 58, p. 164.
62. Ibid., p. 104.
63. Wikileaks, "A/S Boucher Discusses South Asia with the EU," 2 May 2007.
64. Sanchez-Cacideo, n. 36, pp. 134-135.
65. Holt, n. 58, p. 164.
66. Sanchez-Cacicedo, n. 36, p. 122.
67. Remark by Bernard Savage, EU Ambassador to Sri Lanka. Cited in Wikileaks, "Colombo Chiefs of Mission Recommend Ways Forward," 26 February 2010, at http://wikileaks.org/cable/2010/02/10COLOMBO143.html.

68. Sanchez-Cacicedo, n. 36, p. 145.
69. Ibid., p. 149.
70. Holt, n. 58, p. 165.
71. P. Sahadevan, "War and Peace Process," in P. Sahadevan and Neil Devotta, eds., *Politics of Conflict and Peace in Sri Lanka* (New Delhi: Manak, 2006), p. 277; Sumantra Bose, *Contested Lands: Israel-Palestine, Kashmir, Bosinia, Cyprus and Sri Lanka* (Cambridge, Mass.: Harvard University Press, 2007), p. 49.
72. Holt, n. 58, p. 167.

7
Norway and Conflict Resolution in Sri Lanka

Keerthi Sampath Kumar

Throughout its history in conflict resolution, Norway's role in peace efforts has taken different forms which range from acting as an official facilitator of negotiations like in the case of Sri Lanka and the Philippines, to sponsoring secret negotiations such as the Middle East, to being an actor in international coalitions like in Sudan, Ethiopia–Eritrea, Somalia, Colombia and Guatemala.[1]

Norway's ties with Sri Lanka were established through a series of development projects which also helped it to foment personal contacts and visits in Sri Lanka through non-governmental organisations and individuals. Norway's role in the Sri Lankan peace process dates back to the early 1990s when it offered its services to the Sri Lankan Government and the Liberation Tigers of Tamil Eelam (LTTE) in 1991. Subsequently, it deliberately kept a low profile by exploring options for dialogue between the government and the LTTE in order to protect the fragile peace process. Norway maintained special links and access to the inner circles of the LTTE which eventually helped it to become one of the few actors on the international scene that had contacts with and knowledge about the LTTE.[2] Though no major breakthrough was achieved in the initial years, Norway was kept informed about the process through Arne Fjortoft, a former Norwegian politician, who acted as a constant communication channel. Norway expressed its interest to play a role in a possible peace process on the condition that both parties to the conflict requested for the same.[3] In 1995, it dispatched representatives to serve on the proposed monitoring committees that were set up after the 'Cessation of Hostilities Agreement' which was reached between the LTTE and the Kumaratunga government. Its formal role as a mediator emerged only after several years of limited success achieved by peace-building efforts that were carried out by NGOs and civil society groups at the grassroots level.[4]

Defining Conflict Resolution and Third-Party Intervention

Before evaluating the role of Norway in conflict resolution in Sri Lanka, it becomes essential to understand what the terms 'conflict resolution' and 'third-party intervention' mean. Conflict resolution implies that the deep-rooted sources of conflict are addressed and resolved, which further implies that behaviour is no longer violent, attitudes are no longer hostile and the structure of conflict has been changed.[5] Conflict resolution can be defined as "a situation where the conflicting parties enter into an agreement that solves their central incompatibilities, accept each other's continued existence as parties and cease all violent action against each other".[6]

Miall and others argue that the aim of conflict resolution is not the elimination of conflict but to transform actual or potential violent conflict into peaceful (non-violent) processes of social and political change. The objectives of conflict resolution include conflict prevention (the incompatibility of positions of the parties should not escalate to open violence), conflict transformation (the positions of the parties have to be made more compatible), international conflict management (external actors have to contain the escalation of conflict and create incentives for a settlement) and conflict settlement (the parties should reach an agreement on a common institutional framework).[7] However, peace settlements are not "self-executing" but they are sustained best by the work of third parties, external actors who combine mediation, problem-solving and peace-building strategies. These third parties are crucial because they provide the cement to hold things together and provide the creativity, incentives and pressure needed to prevent the parties in conflict from running aground.[8] Tom Woodhouse argues that the "third party intervention following non-violent principles and conflict resolution strategies can work, even if success may be partial and failures may dominate".[9] The entry of the third party changes the conflict structure and allows a different pattern of communications, enabling the third party to filter or reflect back the messages, attitudes and behaviour of the conflictants.[10]

When third parties intervene, there are no neutrals. However, "parties do expect judiciousness—that they can trust the intervenor, that they can rely on that person's judgement, that they can trust the intervenor to carry to the other party what they could not themselves carry because they would lose face or show vulnerability". For third-party intervention to be effective, three conditions must be fulfilled: one, willingness to negotiate or engage in some form of problem-solving on the part of the parties; two, availability of a forum that is agreeable to the parties involved and three, concerns about the credibility of the intervenor.[11]

Having defined what conflict resolution and third-party intervention mean, the following sections will analyse the series of events that unravelled which will throw light on the success or failure of Norway's role in conflict resolution in Sri Lanka. The following sections will analyse Norway's performance through the triple role it played in Sri Lanka: as a facilitator, as one of the monitors of a mission, and as an aid donor.

Norway's Role in the Sri Lankan Peace Process

Role as the Facilitator

Norway gained official recognition for its peace efforts only when President Kumaratunga publicly announced Norway's status as a facilitator in 1999 and it was called to initiate dialogue with the LTTE that was still a banned organisation under Sri Lankan law. Due to the failure of the peace processes in the past, a need for an intermediary was realised and the government for the first time considered third-party facilitation.[12] Thus, with the entry of Norway as a third party, the Sri Lankan conflict turned from a "dyadic conflict" to a "triadic relationship".[13] The selection of Norway as a third party by the government is significant as it was viewed as a country with no overriding interests or leverage. On the other hand, the LTTE viewed and accepted Norway as a mediator. According to the LTTE, it as a state actor was more powerful than an informal mediator or an NGO that was willing to engage them.

Norway was invited by the Government of Sri Lanka (GOSL) and the LTTE and it played an important, supportive role in the Sri Lankan peace process. The acceptance of Norway as a third party is viewed as a reflection of the convergence of interests among the primary parties. Some observers argue that Norway would not have been given a mandate to negotiate without the Indian consent as any solution to the Sri Lankan conflict had to be endorsed by India for it to be successful.[14] Moreover, Norway as a choice for mediation also stemmed from India's hegemonic interests.[15]

Norway was clear about the role that it was going to play—a supportive role where it would not impose anything on either party. Norway was not only the sole facilitator in the Sri Lankan process but was also a joint monitor of the Ceasefire Agreement that was signed in 2002. Unlike its involvement in other peace processes, Norway decided not to work through NGO proxies in Sri Lanka and the Ministry of Foreign Affairs took direct responsibility.

There are several reasons that explain Norway's role in the Sri Lankan peace process. In a 2005 speech delivered by Jon Hanssen Bauer, former Senior Adviser with the Norwegian Ministry of Foreign Affairs, six features of the "Norwegian model" for conflict resolution were enumerated. Firstly, Norway is known for being a "patient facilitator" with the ability to remain engaged even during difficult stages in a peace process. Secondly, it has the necessary resources and domestic political backing for peace and reconciliation processes. Thirdly, Norway cooperates with both national and international NGOs. Fourthly, the peace processes that Norway had been involved in included interaction between diplomatic and humanitarian assistance and between the government and non-state actors. Its engagement in peace processes is accompanied by development cooperation with both state and non-state actors.

Fifthly, there is a widespread opinion that Norway is impartial; with a long tradition for peace that emphasises the ownership of the process by the primary parties. The country is also perceived as a "peace-helper" and not a peace-maker or mediator. Finally, Norway's close relations with other mediators who have international strength and leverage, globally or regionally, are seen as an important asset.[16] In addition to the above reasons, it is argued that peacemaking and reconciliation are the cornerstones of Norwegian foreign policy. It is also viewed as a country with limited geo-strategic interests and no colonial baggage.

Nonetheless, the motives behind its role as a third-party mediator go beyond idealism.[17] Norway has a sizable Tamil population and other than the comparative advantages associated with mediation activities, the peacemaking agenda is an integral aspect of Norway's self-perception and its international image. Norway has been able to promote its national interests by gaining reputation as a "skilled and effective peacemaker". Hoglund and Svensson argue that Norway's involvement in conflict-torn areas has provided it access to key centres of power such as the World Bank, Washington D.C., Brussels and New Delhi. Its interest in acting as a peacemaker in Sri Lanka was also related to its aspiration to be a significant voice in the international system.[18] It has also been able to deploy its soft power through dialogue and facilitation and is associated with "secrecy, flexibility and informality".[19]

The GOSL was clear that Norway was involved in the peace process as a "facilitator" and not as a "mediator". The government was of the opinion that a facilitating role was better aligned with the government's interest to maintain sovereignty.[20] In an interview to *Frontline* magazine, the then Foreign Minister, Lakshman Kadirgamar stated that Norway had a limited role in the peace process. He added,

> a third party's role is limited. It is limited to bringing the two parties together. Shuttling back and forth between the parties. Carrying messages. And laying the groundwork for them to meet.

> There are logistical things they will have to attend to, in due course. There will be venues and times and schedules and various things of that kind. But when it comes to substantive negotiation, the Norwegians will have no particular role at all. . . They will have no mandate to propose solutions. They will certainly have no mandate to make any judgemental decisions. In that sense, they're not arbitrators, they're not judges, they're not mediators.[21]

In the same interview, the Foreign Minister spelt out the reasons for choosing Norway as the third party. One, as a small country, Norway had no agenda of its own. Two, it is geographically far from South Asia and distance has its advantages. Three, Norway has no colonial baggage and lastly, Norway's past experience with peace processes.

The Norwegians referred to themselves as "facilitators" who acted on the "invitation" of the parties. Norway's role included facilitating the peace process, by assisting the parties. It also served as a channel of communication between the parties, either through shuttle diplomacy or by facilitating direct meetings. Its role was also significant in finding venues for the six rounds of peace talks held between September 2002 and March 2003. Other than this, Norway also played an important role in garnering international support for the peace process from the United States, the European Union and Japan and convinced the international community to commit funds for reconstruction and development. On the other hand, the LTTE wanted Norway to play a mediating role which would in turn give them greater credibility.

In the initial years of its involvement in the Sri Lankan peace process, Norway made it clear that a solution to the conflict needs to be sought within a unified Sri Lanka. In 2001, though Norway tried to convince the government to accept bilateral cessation of hostilities, violence continued in the country. At this juncture, Norway realised its limited leverage and tried to establish a supportive international "group of friends" by identifying India and the United States as key players. In the meantime, due to dissatisfaction of

President Kumaratunga, there was a change in the leadership of the Norwegian team: Erik Solheim, a Norwegian MP was replaced by State Secretary Raymond Johansen and later by Vidar Helgesen after the 2001 elections in Norway. These changes, it is argued, damaged Norway's relations with both the parties and Norwegian peace efforts in Sri Lanka began on a difficult note. By the end of 2001, unilateral armistices were in place and negotiations for a more comprehensive and mutual Ceasefire Agreement (CFA) began. The negotiations were supported by the government's peace secretariat, the Secretariat for Coordination of the Peace Process (SCOPP) that was created in February 2002. Norway's shuttle diplomacy, between Ambassador Westborg in Colombo and Solheim's close contacts with LTTE's Anton Balasingham helped in ironing out issues in the Agreement. On the other hand, Norwegian military experts aided in working out the military technicalities of de-escalation and issues related to advanced positions and front lines.[22]

The Ceasefire Agreement that was eventually signed on 22 February 2002 put together preceding humanitarian measures with detailed military arrangements and covered a wide range of issues. It stipulated the following:

- The total cessation of all military action by the Sri Lankan Army and the LTTE, including the cessation of firing of direct and indirect weapons, armed raids, ambushes, assassinations, abductions, destruction of civilian and military property. Parties were to also initiate confidence-building measures to bring normalcy to the country.
- The Sri Lankan Army was to safeguard the sovereignty and the territorial integrity of Sri Lanka without resorting to offensive operations against the LTTE.
- Establishment of the Sri Lankan Monitoring Mission (SLMM) to enquire into violation of the CFA by the conflicting groups. The SLMM would comprise representatives from the Nordic countries.
- It also stipulated provisions for amending or modifying the agreement.[23]

Despite its shortcomings, the CFA was a comprehensive agreement that encompassed a large number of civilian and human rights issues and overcame sticking points that caused trouble in the 1995 truce and the LTTE's unilateral ceasefire in 2000-2002. It was an unprecedented agreement in the Sri Lankan context. However, President Kumaratunga disapproved of Norway overstepping its mandate by adopting a mediator role and introduced a monitoring mission. The signing of CFA without its consent was seen as undemocratic and unconstitutional.[24] But in Norway's assessment, the need for maintaining momentum trumped the need for creating a broader support base and therefore it decided to take an incremental approach with the ceasefire by focusing on humanitarian needs and normalisation.[25]

In the initial stages, the CFA had positive ramifications for the LTTE as it began to consolidate its influence and increase its propaganda, thus violating parts of the agreement. On the other hand, the government slowed down its momentum of implementing the agreement. Though these violations of the CFA raised serious questions about the commitment of both the parties, a positive atmosphere prevailed and expectations from the agreement were high.

A series of formal negotiations were held across Asia and Europe which received domestic and international attention and served symbolic and public diplomacy purposes. Despite Norway's efforts to "keep up the good spirit",[26] there was a lack of hard political issues being brought to the negotiating table. The Oslo Communique that put "federalism" on paper, calling for a federal structure within a united Sri Lanka brought Norway's mediation efforts to a whole new level.

However, the negotiations dwindled when the LTTE witnessed internal discords and the government became increasingly critical of the ceasefire violations. Simultaneously, public support for Norwegian peace efforts and the SLMM diminished and media and opposition parties within Sri Lanka staged protests in front of the Norwegian Embassy in Colombo.

In order to preserve the momentum, a new donor conference was scheduled in Japan to strengthen international support and to generate incentives for the parties. However, the LTTE suspended its participation in the peace talks, citing its exclusion from the Washington conference among other reasons but expressed no intention of terminating the talks. While the government and the international donors proceeded with their meetings as scheduled, the LTTE travelled around the world garnering support. Norway continued to remain in close touch with both the government and the LTTE. One positive outcome of the Japan conference was the creation of three Co-Chairs to the meeting, Japan, the US and the EU along with Norway. The three Co-Chairs expressed their support to the Norwegian efforts and encouraged parties to seek a negotiated settlement. But the donors became increasingly critical of the LTTE than of the government and Norway was left to struggle with dissent among the Co-Chairs.

Towards the end of 2003, the peace talks were put on hold when there was a gradual transformation in Sri Lankan politics and Norway waited for political clarity to emerge in Colombo. Simultaneously, Norway tried to keep the LTTE engaged and maintained its international network. With the deadlock in peace talks, international support to the process withered away. India refused to take on a more overt role, America's anti-terrorism discourse did not yield results, Japan was hesitant to play an active role and the EU did not play a significant role. At this juncture, Norway took stock of its performance and came out with an internal strategy document in January 2004 to review its performance. The document identified international support, a pro-active media policy and the preservation of the military balance as areas of concern. It envisioned itself as a "peace architect" and prioritised challenges such as addressing CFA violations, bringing about economic progress in the north and the east, establishing contact with LTTE, India and other political parties within Sri Lanka on a daily basis, generating pressure from international actors among others.

The split within the LTTE in March 2004 led to political fragmentation and proved to be destabilising. Norway decided to target influential actors to make a difference to the peace process; it invited the parties to review the CFA and insisted on a written confirmation from the GOSL and the LTTE that they wanted Norway to continue its efforts. While Norway was frustrated with the lack of progress, violence escalated in the east. Meanwhile, Norway's shuttle diplomacy continued and it tried to even out contentious issues.

The assassination of Sri Lanka's Foreign Minister Kadirgamar in August 2005 was condemned by international players and the EU considered proscribing the LTTE and suspended its delegations with immediate effect. Norway expressed its discontent with the proposed ban and concluded that the EU ban would impede its role as a facilitator and not be conducive to possibilities of peace. The assassination also sparked off further criticism from the Muslim and Sinhala communities towards the perceived Norwegian appeasement of the LTTE. With increased protests in the country, Norway reviewed its role and contemplated the possibility of "freezing" its facilitation or pulling back for a period.

On assuming office in November 2005, President Mahinda Rajapaksa stated the government's willingness to start a new process through direct talks with the LTTE and avoided any mention of Norway and instead considered the option of facilitation through the UN, India or another regional power. Given the lack of feasible alternatives to replace Norway, both the LTTE and the Rajapaksa government accepted continued Norwegian involvement. Norway, on the other hand, feared the risk of being manipulated and therefore posed three conditions for its involvement—a direct meeting with LTTE leader, Prabhakaran every three months; that the government should cease to undermine Norway's role and commitment from the parties to carry the peace process forward.[27]

Neither party was ready to abrogate the CFA and start war and Norway managed to resume talks in Geneva in February 2006. At the meeting, both the parities extracted unrealistic promises from the opponent and soon after, the SLMM concluded that neither promise was met. Subsequent efforts by Norway to bring the LTTE to the negotiating table failed. Hostilities resumed between the parties; the attempted suicide attack on Army Chief Sarath Fonseka marked a new level of violence in the conflict. Norway managed to make some progress with SCOPP through a joint plan but was left frustrated when the government did not subscribe to the plan.[28] In the subsequent months, Canada and the EU banned the LTTE and Norway remained the only country of the four Co-Chairs willing to meet with the LTTE. This was followed by a long period of "no-war-no-peace" and large scale, territorial offensives resumed in July 2006.[29] When faced with the dilemma of whether or not to remain involved, Norway decided to stay engaged and foresaw its role as limiting the adverse impacts of war. It also applied pressures on the parties about humanitarian concerns and supported humanitarian initiatives.

When Norway realised that the government was engaged in a full-scale war, it decided to take no new initiatives unless the parties reconfirmed their readiness to resume negotiations. The then Norwegian Special Envoy, Hanssen Bauer, offered to withdraw the SLMM and close support to the peace secretariats. But both parties asked Norway to maintain its support to the Peace Secretariat and the SLMM and in fact, they requested Norway to expand the number of monitors. While one section within Norway contemplated withdrawal from Sri Lanka, another was in favour of continued involvement and argued that their departure would not have any positive effect but will only fuel further escalation of conflict. Norway's continued presence also became necessary to address humanitarian concerns and to also preserve its reputation as a persistent and patient mediator.[30]

With violence escalating, humanitarian concerns too rose and four players, viz. the United Nations, the United States, the International Committee of the Red Cross (ICRC) and Norway coordinated their efforts closely. To avoid further bloodshed during the final phases of the war, Norway and the US made several diplomatic attempts and agreed to work towards some form of an LTTE surrender. In February 2009, the LTTE sent a letter to the four Co-Chairs asking them to request for a ceasefire. In response, the international actors called on the LTTE to lay down weapons. Norway, which was in close contact with the United States, continued its efforts to resolve the humanitarian crisis and explored possibilities of some form of LTTE surrender. When an LTTE surrender became a less attractive option for Colombo and other non-Western countries supported the defeat of the LTTE, the Sri Lanka government terminated Norway's role as facilitator in the country and all measures to get the government to agree to internationally monitored safe havens failed.

Role as a Monitor—The SLMM

The GOSL, the LTTE and India insisted on having a small, unarmed monitoring mission with a weak mandate. They also opposed the involvement of major powers such as the EU or a NATO member and preferred a solely Norwegian mission. Norway, however, broadened the mission to include four other countries, realising the dangers of becoming the sole mediator and the sole monitor. The SLMM was to monitor the implementation of the CFA and the head of the mission was to be appointed by Norway. It was further tasked with inquiring into alleged violations of the agreement. Norway also made the largest contributions to the SLMM in terms of finance and personnel.

Hoglund highlights the uniqueness of the SLMM: one, it was entirely Nordic, drawing staff from Norway, Sweden, Denmark, Finland and Iceland. Two, it was a creation of the conflicting parties themselves and was not linked to an international organisation. Three, in spite of being independent, the SLMM was linked to the lead facilitator.[31] Though the mission was small, it was organised and worked for nearly a decade in the sensitive border areas between the warring parties. The positive effects that the mission produced include—one, it registered, processed and made rulings on a large number of cases. It also became a valuable source of observation in the north-east. Two, it managed to boost public confidence during the initial phase of the CFA. Three, the SLMM was able to resolve issues that cropped up at the local levels.[32]

Due to the dual role of Norway, both as a facilitator and the head of the monitoring mission, there was no clarity in the division of its role which became problematic in situations where the SLMM was considered to be biased owing to its connections with Norway.[33] Not only Norway, but the SLMM too played a dual role which led to further ambiguity which became a cause of concern for the mission. While it was mandated to make rulings on cease-fire violations, it was also assigned the duty of working with parties to "resolve any disputes regarding the implementation" of the agreement.[34]

When the EU banned the LTTE, it had negative ramifications especially for the SLMM and the possibility of escalating dynamics of violence. With the escalating conflict, the SLMM did not prove to be effective as it could only inquire into the violations—it neither had the mandate nor the capacity to carry out investigations. After the EU ban, the LTTE issued a deadline for the removal of monitors from EU Member States and subsequently, Denmark, Finland and Sweden withdrew their monitors. Though Iceland increased its personnel contribution, it barely had more people available. Oslo managed to add some staff but was reluctant to fill all the vacancies.

Subsequently, the mission's presence in the field became very limited and was no longer capable of monitoring the incidents and the attacks that followed. The SLMM struggled with issues of asymmetry and neutrality and was also criticised for being biased towards the LTTE. The SLMM recruited and trained personnel on an ad hoc basis and was also at times insufficiently professional and not well-coordinated. Another drawback of the mission was the lack of high-tech intelligence and technological means to take thorough assignments. The SLMM ended up playing second fiddle and became a lame duck. It did not have influence on the turn of events nor could it play a major role in determining the military calculus of the parties. It also failed to bring about reductions in CFA violations which eventually undermined the peace process and the role of the Norwegians.[35]

Role as a Donor: Norwegian Aid to Sri Lanka

Foreign aid became a crucial aspect of the peace process in two respects: one, to create a tangible "peace dividend" and two, to revive the economy and help the government implement its economic reform agenda. With the entry of the CFA, both the government and the LTTE prioritised development and reconstruction over conflict resolution. The Post-Tsunami Operational Management Structure (P-TOMS) was established with Norwegian facilitation to disburse aid in the north and the east. This became an important step to rebuild trust between the government and the LTTE. However, this initiative met with opposition from other communities within Sri Lanka and the provision of economic benefits resulted in a failed effort at conflict resolution.[36]

Norway disbursed a total of US$320 million to Sri Lanka during the period of 1997-2009. Its cooperation during the period was based on two pillars—namely, peace and reconciliation and economic development. It used its aid to Sri Lanka as an enabling mechanism and public diplomacy tool in support of its peace efforts. It is argued that the "peace through development" strategy largely undermined the peace efforts. During the initial days of Norwegian involvement in Sri Lanka, it was recommended that the bulk of Norwegian assistance be discontinued as the government was seen as being responsible for the escalation of the conflict. However, no changes were made to the aid programme as it had a positive impact on development.

In 1997, in an effort to contribute to a peaceful resolution of the conflict, Norway decided to include political development into the development cooperation. In 1998, in the guidelines that were adopted among other aspects, Norway confirmed that all new cooperation proposals would be reviewed on the basis of contribution to the cessation of conflict, to reconciliation and to the search for lasting peace and in this regard, it laid greater emphasis on cooperation with the north and the east.

When the Ceasefire Agreement was signed, Norway increased its aid allocation efforts to link development cooperation to the peace process. From an aid contribution of US$13 million in 1999, it almost doubled in 2003 in line with the CFA and this further doubled to about US$62 million after the 2004 tsunami. The proportion of Norwegian resources allocated to "peace, democracy and human rights" rose from 10.5 per cent in 1997 to 37.7 per cent in 2004. Norway also supported peace-building efforts through civil society organisations. However, Norway realised the conflicting interests in combining the roles of facilitator, donor and monitor and therefore did not actively participate in donor coordination to protect its neutrality.[37]

Evaluation of Norway's Role

Norway's involvement in Sri Lanka as a peace-broker strengthened the momentum towards peace. For the first time in the history of the Sri Lankan conflict, Norway as an independent mediator gained the confidence of both parties. International support and official invitation from the Kumaratunga government granted Norway considerable legitimacy in Sri Lanka.[38] The Norwegian efforts laid the foundation for future dialogue and solutions. The most striking feature in the peace process was the continuous involvement and mediation by Norway to carry out dialogue between both the parties thus bridging the communication gap, and the validity of the CFA despite various instances of violence.[39]

Norway's role in the Sri Lankan peace process was commended for brokering the Ceasefire Agreement which to a considerable extent reduced direct confrontation between both the parties. It was also instrumental in directing the attention and wider engagement of the international community towards Sri Lanka. The agreement not only saved a substantial number of lives, but it also positively affected the conditions for all civilians. Sri Lanka's former Foreign Minister Mangala Samaraweera said: "after two decades of civil war during which more than 65,000 people were killed, the CFA certainly reduced the violence. But most importantly, it gave the LTTE the cloak of political responsibility which they yearned and lacked for years".[40]

Norway was not successful in mediating the conflict as it could not secure peace and Sri Lanka gradually slipped back into an all-out war in 2004. Norwegian efforts were unable to slow "the mobilisation of fighters, open alternative policy windows, provide a signalling mechanism to trigger reciprocal action nor build trust among opponents".[41]

The neutrality of the third party, Norway and SLMM, was a contested issue right from the beginning of the peace process. On the other hand, it was criticised for being too lax in its responses to the human rights abuses committed by the government as well as the LTTE. Norway's role was questioned by various political parties domestically within Sri Lanka. Though it was President Kumaratunga who had invited the Norwegians, she became increasingly sceptical of their mediation efforts. Norway was criticised for being sympathetic towards non-state actors using armed means to pursue political aims and also for providing safe havens to terrorists from different parts of the world. Some observers also viewed it as an active supporter of the LTTE by giving direct and indirect support to the organisation.[42]

It is argued that the very feature of the Norwegian model of mediation, namely "ownership", proved to be detrimental to the peace process. Hoglund and Svensson argue, "the 'two-party model' with the two main parties' 'owning' the process, ultimately led to reduced legitimacy". As a consequence, the process went into troubled waters and Norwegians failed to prevent further escalation of conflict. Since the mediation efforts were not based on a resolution from the United Nations or any other regional or global organisation, Norway had very little leverage. The high degrees of ownership and internationalisation that characterised the peace process were opposed to each other. Since the two parties "owned" the peace process, it reduced the possibility of influence that the international community could exert on important issues such as respect for human rights and protection of civilians.[43]

Another reason cited for the failure of talks was internationalisation of the conflict which raised mistrust in the LTTE about the entire process and the pressure exerted by international actors often backfired. The listing of the LTTE as a terrorist organisation reduced the possibility of Norway to convince them about the viability of the peace talks. Neither could Norway persuade the LTTE to find alternative solutions to address the Tamil grievances. It also increased the expectations of the government of defeating the LTTE militarily rather than through negotiations.

External factors such as the changed international climate post-9/11 and the counter-terrorism agenda conditioned the result of the peace process. Foreign actors were reluctant to interact with the LTTE which hampered the Norwegian model of negotiating with non-state military actors and thus, Norway became the sole conduit to the LTTE. When in 2006, international policy towards the LTTE shifted towards one of all sticks and no carrots, the even-handedness policy of Norway became flawed. Other external factors such as the non-prioritisation of the Sri Lankan issue in the UN, lack of response from regional actors like India and China and the influence of diaspora elements worked against the Norwegian mediation strategy.[44] As Vidar Helgesen remarked in 2007, "Norway is caught between international anti-terrorism policies which it cannot influence and peace diplomacy ambitions it cannot live up to" and "is struggling to square the circle of being a loyal team player helping to demonstrate a united international front against terrorism, while at the same time wanting to support negotiated solutions to conflicts in which one party has been labelled a terrorist organisation".[45]

Norway has also been criticised for having limited influence on the content of the negotiation and the issues subject to negotiation. The NGO—University Teachers for Human Rights—had been critical of its marginal influence especially on the issue of recruitment of child soldiers. Detractors also accuse Norway of being impartial in light of the asymmetrical degree of violations of the Ceasefire Agreement. This asymmetry manifested in the violations committed by the LTTE which were more in number than those by the government. According to SLMM reports, during the period between 2002 and 2005, the LTTE committed 96 per cent of the ceasefire violations. The Nordic countries were criticised for turning a blind eye to LTTE violations. It also influenced the perception that Norway was biased in favour of the LTTE.[46] Norway's "evenhandedness" was seen as detrimental to the long-term sustainability of the peace process.[47]

The Ceasefire Agreement also did not address a crucial aspect of the conflict; it failed to recognise the so-called Sea Tigers, the naval unit of the LTTE and thus did not lay down any safeguarding mechanisms that could mitigate situations that could potentially arise at sea.[48] The agreement also failed to formalise the exact front lines, thus was unable to prevent clashes between the Sri Lankan army and the LTTE. Nor did the agreement give power to the SLMM to force compliance to the CFA.[49]

The dual role that Norway assumed—that of a mediator and a monitor—negatively impacted the peace process and created perceptions of bias. Both Norway and the SLMM have been severely criticised for having allowed the LTTE to be involved in the peace process despite their continued violence and human rights abuses instead of being harder on the rebels. This, according to critics, seriously undermined the legitimacy of the SLMM.[50]

Another cause for the failure of the peace process was the bipolar strategy adopted by Norway which was based on the premise of bringing about negotiations between the two armed parties. Such a strategy excluded other legitimate stakeholders in the conflict including the mainstream opposition, the Muslim community, non-LTTE Tamil dissidents, Sinhala nationalists and representatives in the north-east and so on. In the initial days of the peace process, the Norwegian Embassy was perceived to be isolationalist and it was only around 2005, that it began to actively engage a wider group of people.[51]

Despite continuous efforts to broker peace between both the parties, Norway failed. This can be traced to three causes as listed by Madhawa Palihapitiya:

One, the GOSL and the LTTE had different opinions over the role Norway played; while the government saw Norway as a facilitator, the LTTE wanted it to mediate the peace process. Though Norway had limited itself to the role of a facilitator, in practice, it went beyond the passing of messages and logistic arrangements for the peace talks. It was actively involved in framing of the CFA and other documents like the Tsunami Operation Management Structure (P-TOMS) agreement; it influenced discussions and exerted diplomatic pressure on the parties. Therefore, the Norwegians were not only facilitators but also mediators and they switched between these roles. However, the Norwegians were not successful in integrating the different stances of both the parties and the resulting ambiguity gave the government the chance to wage war against the LTTE.

Two, Norway did not have the military and political muscle or the leverage to prevent resumption of the conflict. It could not convince either party that the costs of war were higher than the costs of peace. Thus, it could not encourage them in "mobilisation slowing". After the peace talks unravelled, Norway did not have any leverage and could hardly borrow any from powerful states.[52]

Lastly, in the Sri Lankan context, neither a mutually hurting stalemate existed nor was there a drive for resolution. It is the primary role of the third party to recognise the onset of "ripeness" in a conflict and encourage both the parties to enter into negotiations.[53] Among the four conditions[54] listed for a mutually hurting stalemate to exist, at least one or two of these changes have to take place on the ground. But, it is argued that Norway failed to convince the parties of the existence of a mutually hurting stalemate and it failed to explore the "ripe moment" for conflict resolution.[55]

Conclusion

Though Norwegian efforts to broker peace in Sri Lanka failed, its efforts and achievements cannot be undermined. Through its consistent and sustained efforts, it won respect from the international community. Its successes include the Ceasefire Agreement, the Oslo Declaration, the P-TOMS agreement and the positive economic benefits of this period. The main reasons for the failure of the peace process cannot be sought in the dynamics of third-party efforts alone, but that the structural and personal characteristics of the main parties were equally responsible for the failure of peace talks. The parties showed lack of willingness to seek a compromise, exhibited the inability to integrate the plurality of the society into the process and the growing uncertainty of the power bases of the parties led to lack to progress.[56]

Moreover, observers argue that neither the LTTE nor the GOSL entered into peace talks with a common commitment to a shared vision of peace. Each of them saw it as an opportunity to further their goals—the LTTE wanted some version of Tamil Eelam while the government wanted the preservation of a unitary state.[57] For the first time in Sri Lanka's history, the international community played a predominant role in the peace process. However, by "keeping the space open for conflict resolution and transformation", the international actors failed to transform the roots of hostility nor did they succeed in transforming the local capacities for peace-building.[58] Despite the significant efforts and resources put in by Norway, it neither had the leverage of a powerful mediator nor the support or protection of parties or international partners to prevent the escalation of conflict.

Notes

1. Kjell Magne Bondevik, "Norway—100 years of Independence: Norwegian Foreign Policy and Engagement in International Peace Processes," Speech delivered at Institute of Policy Studies and New Zealand Institute of International Affairs, Victoria University, Wellington, 14 March 2005.
2. Kristine Hoglund and Isak Svensson, "Mediating between Tigers and Lions: Norwegian Peace Diplomacy in Sri Lanka's Civil War," *Contemporary South Asia*, 17(2), 2009, p. 180.
3. Norwegian Agency for Development Cooperation (NORAD), Norwegian Ministry of Foreign Affairs, *Pawns of Peace: Evaluation of Norwegian Peace Efforts in Sri Lanka, 1997-2009*, Report 5/2011, p. 29.
4. John Stephen Moolakkattu, "Peace Facilitation by Small States: Norway in Sri Lanka," *Cooperation and Conflict*, 40(4), 2005, p. 390.
5. Hugh Miall, et al., *Contemporary Conflict Resolution: The Prevention, Management and Transformation of Deadly Conflicts* (Cambridge: Polity Press, 1999), p. 21.
6. Peter Wallensteen, *Understanding Conflict Resolution: War, Peace and the Global System* (London: Sage Publishers, 2007), p. 8.
7. Bruno Coppieterss, "The EU and Georgia: Time Perspectives in Conflict Resolution," *Occasional Paper*, No. 70 (Paris: European Union Institute for Security Studies, 2007), p. 27.

8. Fen Olser Hampson, *Nurturing Peace: Why Peace Settlements Succeed or Fail* (Washington, D.C.: United States Institute of Peace, 1996), p. viii.
9. Tom Woodhouse, *International Conflict Resolution: Some Critiques and a Response*, Working Paper 1, University of Bradford, 1999, pp. 17-18.
10. See Miall, n. 5, p. 9.
11. James H. Laue, "The Emergence of Institutionalisation of Third-party Roles in Conflict," in John Burton and Frank Dukes, eds., *Conflict: Readings in Management and Resolution* (London: Macmillan, 1960), pp. 260, 267-268.
12. Mari Saifuddin Effendi, "Role of Third Party in Conflict Resolution: A Case Study of India and Norway in Sri Lanka," *RCSS Policy Studies*, 41 (Colombo: Regional Centre for Strategic Studies, 2007), p. 59.
13. Jacob Bercovitch, "Introduction: Thinking about Mediation," in Jacob Bercovitch, ed., *Resolving International Conflict: The Theory and Practice of Mediation* (Boulder, CO: Lynne Rienner, 1996). Quoted in John Stephen Moolakkattu, "Peace Facilitation by Small States: Norway in Sri Lanka," *Cooperation and Conflict*, 40(4), 2005, p. 386.
14. See Wallensteen, n. 6, p. 181.
15. Madhawa Palihapitiya, "Of a Norwegian Summer and a Viking Intervention in Sri Lanka," *Asian Journal of Public Affairs*, 1(1), 2007, p. 42.
16. Jon Hanssen-Bauer, "The Norwegian 'Model' for Conflict Resolution," speech delivered at Lisbon, 28 October 2005.
17. Alan Bullion, "Norway and the Peace Process in Sri Lanka," *Civil Wars*, 4(3), 2001, p. 77.
18. See Wallensteen, n. 6, pp. 179 and 186.
19. See Coppieterss, n. 7, p. 4.
20. Eric Brahm, "Sovereignty," in Guy Burgess and Heidi Burgess, eds., *Beyond Intractability,* Conflict Research Consortium, University of Colorado, Boulder, 2004. Quoted in Madhawa Palihapitiya, "Of a Norwegian Summer and a Viking Intervention in Sri Lanka," *Asian Journal of Public Affairs*, 1(1), 2007, p. 43.
21. N. Ram, "I Can Confirm that the Peace Process is Moving", Interview with Foreign Minister Lakshman Kadirgamar, *Frontline*, 18(8), 14-27 April 2001 [Online web] URL:http://www.flonnet.com/fl1808/18081230.htm (accessed on 19 January 2013).
22. See Coppieterss, n. 7, pp. 34-36.
23. See Woodhouse, n. 9, p. 61.
24. A. Fernando, *My Belly is White* (Colombo: Vijitha Yapa Publications, 2008). Quoted in Norwegian Agency for Development Cooperation, n. 3, p. 37.
25. See Coppieterss, n. 7, pp. 37-38.
26. Ibid., p. 39.
27. See ibid., p. 57.
28. The joint plan proposed substantive political discussions in three phases: 1) strengthen the CFA and start negotiations, 2) devise interim arrangements to facilitate the return of normalcy, and 3) reach agreement on a permanent solution.
29. See Coppieterss, n. 7, p. 60.
30. Ibid., p. 62.
31. Kristine Hoglund, "Obstacles to Monitoring: Perceptions of the Sri Lanka

Monitoring Mission and the Dual Role of Norway," *International Peacekeeping*, 18(2), 2011, p. 211.
32. See Coppieterss, n. 7, pp. 100-101.
33. See ibid., p. 212.
34. Kristine Hoglund, and Isak Svensson, "'Damned if You Do, and Damned if You Don't: Nordic Involvement and Images of Third-Party Neutrality in Sri Lanka," *International Negotiation*, 13, 2008, p. 351.
35. See Coppieterss, n. 7, pp. 98-100 and 104-106.
36. Ibid., pp. 107-109.
37. J.D. Whaley, C. Orjuela and K. Stokke with P. Bauck, "How Cooperation can Support the Peace Process in Sri Lanka—An assessment of Norwegian Development Cooperation and Options for the Future," Report to Ministry of Foreign Affairs, NORAD and the Royal Norwegian Embassy in Colombo, 2006. Quoted in Norwegian Agency for Development Cooperation, n. 3, pp. 112 and 117.
38. Kristine Hoglund, and Isak Svensson, "The Peace Process in Sri Lanka," *Civil Wars*, 5(4), 2002, p. 112.
39. See Woodhouse, n. 9, p. 64.
40. Ibid., p. 77.
41. See Bondevik, n. 1, p. 5.
42. See Wallensteen, n. 6, p. 182.
43. Ibid., pp. 184 and 186.
44. See ibid., pp. 76, 80
45. Vidar Helgesen, "How Peace Diplomacy Lost Post 9/11: What Implications are There for Norway?," *Oslo Files on Defence and Security*: 2007, p. 14.
46. See Coppieterss, n. 7, p. 350
47. Alan Keenan, "The Trouble with Evenhandedness: On the Politics of Human Rights and Peace Advocacy in Sri Lanka," in M. Feher, *Nongovernmental Politics* (Brooklyn, NY: Zone Books, 2007). Quoted in Kristine Hoglund and Isak Svensson, "Mediating between Tigers and Lions: Norwegian Peace Diplomacy in Sri Lanka's Civil War," *Contemporary South Asia*, 17(2), 2009, p. 185.
48. See Coppieterss, n. 7, p. 349.
49. See ibid., pp.95-96.
50. Kristine Hoglund, "Violence and the Peace Process in Sri Lanka," *Civil* Wars, 7(2), 2005, p. 167.
51. See Coppieterss, n. 7, pp. 88, 89.
52. Ibid., p. 74.
53. See NORAD, n. 3, p. 73.
54. The four conditions include failed tactics, depletion of available resources to fuel the conflict, a resolution in support of the conflict by the members or the allies or the costs becoming too high to continue.
55. See Bondevik, n. 1, pp. 43-46.
56. See Coppieterss, n. 7, p. 356.
57. Ibid., p. 81.
58. Jonathan Goodhand, et al. *Aid, Conflict and Peace-building in Sri Lanka, 2000-2005* (Colombo: The Asia Foundation, 2005), p. 72.

8
The EU, India and Conflict Resolution in Myanmar: Is there a Space for Cooperation?

Patryk Kugiel

In the last two decades, the policies of the European Union and India towards Myanmar have often been a source of tension and misunderstanding between the two strategic partners. While the Union adopted a restrictive approach and sided unanimously with the Opposition in Myanmar against the military junta, India has eventually opted for a more pragmatic policy of modest engagement with the official government. This has led to disappointment in Brussels and other Western capitals. Any cooperation between the two to support Myanmar efforts at peace and internal reconciliation were apparently out of question. These disagreements are based on fundamental strategic and ideological differences. They would have probably continued indefinitely in the near future as an irritant in bilateral relations had Myanmar not entered into a process of rapid political and economic transformations since 2011. The unprecedented reforms unfolding there offer new opportunities for cooperation between the EU and India as well as other European countries.

This chapter examines the evolution and comparison of Indian and EU policies towards Myanmar in the last two decades and highlights the reasons behind existing differences. It discusses recent changes and urges both India and the European Union to cooperate in supporting conflict resolution in the country. Although examples of Indo-European joint initiatives in third countries are rather limited and new disagreements may possibly emerge between the two in the future over economic and security interests, Myanmar offers an interesting area for cooperation. The sooner India and the Union recognise their complimentary interests and the potential for common actions in Myanmar, the better it would be for the troubled country as well as the EU–India strategic partnership.

Divergent Approaches, 1988-2010

Mainly because of its self-imposed isolationist policy, Myanmar had not emerged as an important partner for neither India nor the European Communities during the Cold War. Despite close links between pro-independence leaders in India and Myanmar—Jawaharlal Nehru and Aung San—and cooperation during the early years after independence, relations between the two deteriorated in the aftermath of the military coup of General Ne Win in 1962, amidst the expulsion of many Indians from the country and growing anti-India rhetoric of the new junta. Europe, for its part, never had a strong presence in Myanmar (with the exception of the former colonial power—the United Kingdom). Since Ne Win had closed the country to the outside world, relations focused mostly on development cooperation with several European states with Germany, France, and the UK emerging as major donors.

In the late 1980s, as the dictatorship started opening up to the outside world, both India and Europe were keen to re-engage the country. However, the brutal crackdown on students' protests in August 1988 in which some 3,000 people had been killed and the subsequent military coup in September, which brought to power the new military junta known as the State Law and Order Restoration Council (SLORC), put an end to these hopes. The repression of the opposition and rejection of results of the 1990 general election, in which the opposition National League of Democracy (NLD) led by Aung Sun Suu Kyi was victorious, caused widespread international condemnation and complicated the country's return to the international community. These developments posed a serious challenge for both the EU and India, but over time their responses evolved differently.

The developments of 1988 marked the beginning of a hardline position of Western Europe on Myanmar. The European countries strongly condemned the suppression of the democratic movement by the military regime and stopped all development cooperation programmes, except for strictly humanitarian aid. After a new wave of repressions following the 1990 elections, the European Commission imposed a strict arms embargo on Myanmar. A year later, European countries expelled Myanmar's military personnel from the country's embassies in Europe, withdrew their military attachés from Rangoon and ended all military and security cooperation. At the same time, the Europeans offered full support to the imprisoned NLD leader Aung San Suu Kyi, who was awarded the Sakharov Prize for Freedom of Thought by the European Parliament in 1991. Later that year, she also received the Nobel Peace Prize.

Reflecting the new institutional setting under the Treaty of Maastricht, the European Union endorsed the Common Position on Burma on 28 October 1996. It basically renewed the arms embargo, the suspension of military cooperation and development assistance, and added a ban of high-level political contacts and visa restrictions on military personnel and their families.[1] The Common Position became the main document guiding the policy of the EU and its Member States towards Myanmar. It was annually reinforced and expanded with the addition of more members of the military regime being added to the blacklist and renewed restrictions on trade and investment.

In October 1997, as one of the most substantial coercive measures, the EU suspended Myanmar from preferential trade access to European market, viz. the Generalized Scheme of Preferences (GSP). In 2001, when the Union initiated a special tariff-free and quota-free scheme for the Least Developed Countries (LDCs), known as "Everything but Arms" (EBA), Myanmar was excluded from the list of beneficiaries. This has led to a significant reduction of economic cooperation in recent years, with a miniscule value of trade at €312 million in 2011. Today, all 28 EU Member States account for a meagre 2 per cent of Myanmar's total foreign trade. Myanmar is ranked at 141st position among EU major trade partners.[2] Similarly,

EU sanctions hampered European interest to invest in the country. Thus, after imposing sanctions in the 1990s, "actual inflows from the European Union (EU) have slowed, though they have not dried up completely" with several projects undertaken especially by France and the United Kingdom.[3]

In the absence of political, economic and military cooperation, the EU renewed limited development cooperation with Myanmar only in the mid-2000s. In 2007, the EU prepared its first multi-annual programme of assistance *(Country Strategy Paper)* for Myanmar and assigned €65 million for projects in two focal sectors, viz. health and education along with small humanitarian packages for Myanmar's refugees in neighbouring countries.[4] EU aid was supplemented by the support of several European countries, which maintained some presence in Myanmar, viz. the UK, Germany, France, Sweden, and Denmark. In the absence of a political or security dialogue with the Myanmar government, any EU role in internal conflict resolution was simply not possible. Hence, for the past two decades EU policy on Myanmar remained focused almost exclusively on democratisation agenda and Aung Sun Suu Kyi with coercive measures as the only tool of influence. As the situation in Myanmar was not improving, the policy of sanctions remained in place until early 2012. Only after serious reforms gained momentum since 2011, a new chapter in EU–Myanmar relations has opened.

India's initial response to developments of 1988 was not very different from to that of Europe. Even though the visit of Prime Minister Rajiv Gandhi to Myanmar in 1987 constituted a step forward in engaging both neighbours, the brutal repression of the students' movement prompted India to condemn the SLORC and offer support to Myanmar dissidents. As one Indian author writes:

> India, during 1988-1991, not only fiercely criticised the military rule in Myanmar and its repressive mechanism against the pro-democracy movement but also very openly supported democratic leaders in material and financial terms in their cause by setting refugee camps along the borders for political activists.[5]

India was also among the strongest advocates of the release of NLD leader Suu Kyi—a graduate of a Delhi College. Apart from providing safe sanctuaries, India allowed Myanmar's opposition National Coalition Government of the Union of Burma (NCGUB) to open an office on Indian territory in 1992 and permitted an independent radio and press to operate from its territory. Bilateral relations deteriorated to the brink of a proxy war, with Indian intelligence services apparently providing financial support for Kachin insurgents and Karen rebels and Myanmar's support for insurgents operating in the Indian Northeast.[6]

It was not until 1991-1992 and the promulgation of the new 'Look East policy' that things started changing and the Indian approach become more pragmatic by seeking re-engagement with the ruling junta. With the adoption of a more realistic foreign policy with the end of the Cold War, a more pragmatic phase in bilateral relations began. Concerns about the growing inroads of China in Myanmar and with no signs of military rulers relinquishing power, India realised that its policy of coercion had failed and that there was no other realistic alternative than to engage with whomsoever ruled Yangon.

A visit by Foreign Secretary J.N. Dixit to Yangon in 1993 paved the way for rebuilding strained ties with the junta and resulted in two agreements for enhancing border trade and controlling drug trafficking. A year later, India signed a Memorandum of Understanding to Maintain Border Tranquility and resumed military cooperation.

After a brief period of tensions in the aftermath of the Indian government's decision to award the Jawaharlal Nehru Award for International Understanding to Aung Sun Suu Kyi in 1995, cooperation was back on track in subsequent years. In 1998, with a new government in New Delhi under Prime Minister Atal Behari Vajpayee, bilateral relations were given "a renewed push".[7] The first high-level visit to India in January 2000 of Senior General Maung Aye, Deputy Chairman of the State Peace and Development Council (successor to SLORC), was followed by two major visits:

that of Senior General Than Shwe, Chairman of SPDC, in October 2004, and of General Maung Aye in 2008. Vice President of India Bhairon Singh Shekhawat visited Myanmar in November 2003 and President A.P.J. Abdul Kalam in March 2006. As an Indian analyst put it: India made "a choice for itself, preferring pragmatism over idealism, and stuck to it despite regime changes in New Delhi".[8] When the Myanmar regime was being highly criticised in the West in anticipation of the general elections in 2010, Prime Minister Manmohan Singh received for the second time the Chairman of SPDC Senior General Than Shwe in Delhi for a five-day visit from 25-29 July. The two leaders reaffirmed their commitment to strengthen cooperation on a number of issues, including countering terrorism, energy, infrastructure development and defence. They also signed additional agreements aimed at tackling the smuggling of arms and drugs across their borders, and cooperation in the field of science and technology.[9] By recalling the Five Principles of Peaceful Coexistence as the basis of bilateral relations, India confirmed its policy of non-interference in the internal affairs of Myanmar.

Both countries also used a regional approach to strengthen cooperation and joined two new institutional arrangements, viz. the Bangladesh-India-Myanmar-Sri Lanka-Thailand Economic Cooperation (BIMSTEC) in 1997 and Mekong–Ganga Cooperation in 2000. Moreover, after Myanmar joined the Association for South East Asian Nations (ASEAN) in 1997, India gained a direct land border with ASEAN. Myanmar was also invited as an Observer to the South Asian Association for Regional Cooperation (SAARC) in 2007. One cannot altogether rule out full membership in the organisation in the forseeable future.

Over the years, India has stepped up cooperation in the field of security, military, and economy with Myanmar and engaged in number of infrastructure and energy projects across the country. India was also admitted as one of the few countries to provide humanitarian assistance in the aftermath of the disastrous Cyclone Nargis in April 2008. Since then, India emerged as one of major foreign aid donors in Myanmar and engaged in several infrastructure, education, energy and technological projects, even though the scale of Indian investments remained below expectations.[10] This approach of growing interaction with ruling junta and apparently symbolic support for the Aung Sun Suu Kyi and democratic movements in Myanmar has continued throughout the first decade of twenty-first century in contrast to Western policy.

Myanmar as a Bone of Contention between India and the European Union

As EU sanctions on Myanmar were being tightened over time, India was enhancing its cooperation with the military regime. India's soft stance on Myanmar regime was not well received in Brussels and other European capitals. This eventually added to the mutual distrust between the two sides. Although no EU leader went so far as to criticise India for not condemning human rights violations in Myanmar as did US President Barack Obama in his speech to the Indian Parliament in November 2010[11], India has found itself under repeated pressure from the EU and its Member States for not doing enough to encourage change in the country. Moreover, European countries were especially critical of India for continuing military cooperation and supplying the Myanmar regime with arms and ammunition. There was growing controversy especially when India was accused of reselling European military equipment to the junta, e.g. in the case of the British-built BN-2 naval surveillance warplanes in 2007[12], or more recently, when Swedish-made M-3 Carl Gustav anti-tank rifles were discovered in Myanmar in late 2012.[13]

From the Western perspective, it was argued that the lack of universal sanctions undermined their effectiveness and as long as countries like China or India continued their trade, investments and psychological support for Myanmar's junta, it would be difficult to bring a real change there.[14] This argument was repeatedly endorsed by the European Parliament, a place traditionally more concerned about human rights than national interests, in a number of its resolutions. For instance, in May 2010 it "urged" India together with China and Russia "to use their considerable economic and political leverage with the Burmese authorities in order to bring about substantial improvements in Burma/Myanmar and to stop supplying the country with weaponry and other strategic resources".[15] The European Parliament raised the problem of Myanmar also on the occasion of preparations for the EU–India Summit in Marseilles in 2008, when it called upon the EU and India "to work together to prevail upon the Burmese military junta to release political prisoners and to respect human rights".[16]

India came under severe criticism, especially from the European civil society and human rights groups with number of reports condemning India for cooperation with the undemocratic regime in Ny Pyi Taw. Europe used to increase its criticism especially during recurring crises in Myanmar. For instance, after the brutal crackdown on protests by monks in 2007, the EU and the United States issued a joint statement urging India alongwith China, the ASEAN and others in the region "to use their influence in support of the people of Burma/Myanmar".[17] Some EU Member States also tried to seek greater support from India for an international mission in Myanmar to foster democratic transformation.[18] Not surprisingly, all those calls fell on deaf ears in New Delhi. EU pressure on India to halt cooperation with the military regime in Myanmar was in those times when the Union enjoyed close relations with number of dictators worldwide including in Egypt, Libya or Pakistan. This was seen in New Delhi as an example of European double standards and hypocrisy in international relations.

As a result, although the situation in Myanmar has been discussed by both sides during annual summits, this did not lead to tangible results except for general declarations in support of "national reconciliation" and "inclusive dialogue".[19] Far from being an area of cooperation and common action, Myanmar has remained a serious irritant in EU–India relations for the last two decades. What seemed to be a rejection of global responsibilities by an emerging power to promote human rights and democracy on the one hand, was perceived as an expression of post-colonial policies by the other. Tensions over the Myanmar policy evolved from both real concerns about the most effective ways of dealing with an undemocratic regime as well as misunderstandings and lack of knowledge about the concerns and compulsions of the other side.

Idealism versus Pragmatism?

India–EU differences regarding Myanmar have often been portrayed as a difference between idealism and pragmatism in foreign relations. However, in fact, they are based on very fundamental differences and divergent national interests between the two sides regarding Myanmar. One of the crucial and obvious differences in approach to Myanmar is dictated by geography.

India, which shares over 1,600 kilometres of a porous border with Myanmar, does not have the luxury like the faraway EU to jeopardise its strategic interests for the sake of human rights and values. Due to geographical proximity, India enjoys strong historical, cultural, religious and civilisational ties with Myanmar. There are around 365,000 people of Indian origin living in Myanmar according to official Indian estimates (though according to other reports the number may be as much as 2.5 million)[20], whose interests must be taken into account when planning policy in New Delhi. Indeed, being located in a difficult neighbourhood where democracy in recent decades has been rather an exception than a rule, India could hardly afford not talking to dictatorships. Geographical distance also helped European societies and politicians to perceive internal problems in Myanmar in a Manichean perspective, as a fight between "good" opposition forces and an "evil" military. This black-and-white approach, as indicated by Michael Aung Twin, allowed for mobilisation of European civil society to support their states' policies, but made any compromise with the Myanmar regime less likely.[21] On the other hand, in neighbouring India there was no such over-simplistic view of Myanmar; there was greater understanding of the complex internal situation in the country. As a result, despite popular sympathy for Aung Sun Suu Kyi, there was never a mass movement in support of the Myanmar opposition's struggle for democracy. As a result, the more pragmatic policy of the government was never seriously contested.

Another reason for India–EU divergences is the different strategic value of Myanmar for the two entities. European countries had no significant economic or security interests in Myanmar prior to 1988. Thereafter, they remained concerned primarily about the humanitarian and human rights situation in the country with extra attention paid to the problem of illicit drugs. Even if some European countries like Germany, France and Italy were willing to explore the vast economic potential of a mineral-rich country in recent years, this was effectively hampered by existing sanctions and the international isolation of Myanmar. On the contrary, India had multifaceted geopolitical, security and economic interests in Myanmar. Although many analysts provide different explanations regarding the main driving force behind the change in India's policy on Myanmar, the following four important interests seems to be the most crucial.

Look East Policy

Myanmar literally stands today on the way of stronger India's engagement in Southeast Asia. It could become a land bridge of India with ASEAN and China, opening up new opportunities for trade and development. With the strong growth in Southeast Asian nations in the 1980s, India started paying more attention to developing good relations with the region and this gave the beginning to India's Look East Policy (LEP) announced in 1991. Nevertheless, as was observed recently by an Indian analyst, "a major lacuna in India's LEP has been the absence of deep engagement with Myanmar, which is not only India's neighbour—sharing a land border with India—but also a gateway for India to ASEAN. Closer engagement with Myanmar will give a boost to India's LEP".[22]

Since the 1990s several projects were discussed and some of them implemented in recent years to improve connectivity between India and Southeast Asia. These include the upgradation of the Tamu-Kalewa-Kalemyoa road (about 160 km) in Myanmar across the border from Manipur; the Kaladan Multi-Modal Transit Transport Project, which envisages development of road and inland waterways from Sittwe port in Myanmar to Mizoram; improvement of Rhi-

Tiddim Road (about 60 km) in Myanmar adjoining Mizoram; and some segments of the Trilateral Highway Project (about 1,360 km) connecting Moreh (Manipur, India) to Mae Sot (Thailand) through Myanmar. However, the impact of those investments on India's connectivity to the ASEAN countries has been limited so far and more efforts are required to make a difference.

Insurgency in the Northeast

Four Indian Northeast states neighbouring Myanmar, viz. Manipur, Tripura, Nagaland and Arunachal Pradesh, have been an area of anti-India insurgencies with many rebel groups taking shelter and supplies across the border. Apart from insurgency, other crucial threats have a cross-border character: drug trafficking, illegal weapons' trade, cross-border migration and economic stagnation. Thus, close military and border cooperation with the Myanmar army is crucial for India's national security and stability.[23]

Moreover, as India' peripheral states, with limited transport connections with the rest of the country and being among the most underdeveloped in India, opening for trade with Southeast Asia through Myanmar was seen as a crucial solution to their problems. New road and rail projects from India's Northeast to China, Thailand and the Bay of Bengal through Myanmar, could enhance India's trade and help to transform this landlocked and secluded part of the country into a prosperous trade and transit hub. As some Indian authors stressed: "In a world which is shrinking constantly, India's Northeast can no longer be considered a buffer against external threats. The development of infrastructure connecting India and Myanmar has acquired its own salience".[24]

Energy Needs

With a fast growing economy and high dependence on imported sources of energy, India's thirst for mineral resources will increase in the years ahead. Myanmar, with its untapped reserves of minerals, especially gas, and geographical proximity has emerged as a critical partner for India's energy security.[25] Since the first agreement on energy was signed in 2003, three Indian companies (two state-owned, viz. the Oil and Natural Gas Corporation (ONGC), and Gas Authority of India, Ltd. (GAIL), and one private company Essar Oil Ltd. (EOL)) has already acquired shares in seven blocks in Myanmar by 2009.[26] Several options for the construction of a gas pipeline have been already discussed. However, the projects are hampered by disagreements between India and Bangladesh, through which territory would be the most feasible way to transport gas. However, India's energy needs will continue to play an important role in shaping the country's policy on Myanmar.

The China Factor

Despite the official rhetoric to the contrary, geopolitical and economic rivalry with China has been one of the main driving forces behind Indian foreign policy in the last two decades. Having a pro-China Pakistan on its western border, India could hardly accept Myanmar in the east being dominated by China, especially when this area was traditionally considered as part of the Indian sphere of influence. Not surprisingly, when China stepped in to fill the international vacuum in Myanmar in the late 1980s, India had to re-evaluate its policy towards Myanmar. Since 1993, as an Indian author observed:

> There has been a significant shift in India's Myanmar policy to counterbalance China's influences there. Much like ASEAN, New Delhi has now decided to follow a policy of 'constructive engagement' with Yangon, thus abandoning its earlier stance of isolating the Myanmar military regime.[27]

One can expect that the China factor will continue to play an important role in shaping India's policy on Myanmar, which witnessed greater Chinese inroads in the last decade.

Finally, apart from all practical and strategic considerations, EU–India disagreements in dealings with Myanmar also evolved from very fundamental ideological differences. Albeit being the world's largest democracy itself, India does not share the EU enthusiasm for democracy promotion, at least in a form it is being done in by the West. As a post-colonial state, India has a limited tolerance for Western lecturing and direct interference in the internal affairs of developing countries. Thus, strategic autonomy, state sovereignty and the principle of non-interference are regarded as cornerstones of Indian foreign policy. Moreover, being the largest country in South Asia, India would like to be viewed as a "benign hegemon" and must be especially cautious when dealing with its neighbours—a principle officially endorsed in Indian foreign policy as the "Gujral doctrine". As a result, even though India and the EU share adherence to the same principles of democracy, human rights and tolerance, they can hardly be found as cooperating in support to democracy anywhere in the world.

All these facts show that the differences between the EU and India regarding Myanmar were real, grounded on a very solid basis and were not to go away. Having pivotal national interests in maintaining good working relations with whomsoever rules in Yangon, rising India was ready to withstand any international criticism and pressure. With a similarly frozen EU hardline policy, the only change could have come from Myanmar itself.

Bridging the Gap since 2011

Top-down reforms initiated in Myanmar in 2003 as a seven-step roadmap to "disciplined democracy" went unnoticed in the West, or assessed as another game played by the generals to hold onto power. However, with the new constitution approved in 2008, general elections held in 2010 and the release of Aung San Suu Kyi soon thereafter, the transformation process gained momentum in 2011. In March 2011, the SDPC transferred power initially to a nominally civilian government headed by former General Thein Sein. Several important reforms were also introduced, viz. the release of political prisoners, the end of censorship of media and a ceasefire with ethnic rebels. When the NLD was allowed to contest the by-election to Parliament in April 2012, the conduct of largely fair elections led to its landslide victory. This led many to conclude that "this time the change that is occurring is substantive, not cosmetic."[28] Even if on-going political and economic reforms were regarded as "incomplete and fragile", they gave both the EU and India a chance to introduce crucial readjustments in their policies.

In fact, neither the EU nor India, although with different approaches, achieved much in attaining their stated objectives. It seems that they were equally ineffective in bringing change in Myanmar. The transformation that occurred was due neither to India's constructive engagement nor to European moralist condemnation, but because of some internal reasons which are not yet fully understood. The so-called leverage and influence of both players in Myanmar were simply too shallow to enforce any changes on the military junta. They were ineffective at best, and costly to all sides at worst. They also created unnecessary tensions in relations between the EU and India.

European coercive policy focused on human rights and democratisation. This has become an object of criticism from many angles, even though credible alternatives were not in sight. There was also growing recognition within the Union that "targeted sanctions" were doing more harm to common citizens rather than to the generals. A visa ban on military elites or freezing assets of members of the junta would hardly affect the generals as long as other Asian countries were open to accept their visits. For instance, the ban on the import of precious gems from Myanmar introduced in 2007 was meaningless as it never constituted an important export item to Europe. Similarly, when Brussels froze assets of blacklisted persons from the military establishment, EU bankers could hardly find more than 70,000. A ban on investment was hardly significant as Myanmar has never been an important destination for EU capital. As one observer of EU's approach noted in 2010: "The past two decades of sanction policies adopted within the EU have failed to achieve their initial objective of promoting and accelerating Burma's democratic transition".[29] The problem with the European policy of carrots and sticks was that it entailed only sticks and no carrots.

The lack of EU leverage over the Myanmar regime was evident when the EU Special Envoy for Burma/Myanmar, Piero Fassino (appointed in November 2007), could not even visit the country as the junta denied him a visa. Similarly, when Cyclone Nargis hit Myanmar in 2008 offers of humanitarian assistance by European countries were spurned by the military regime, leaving European societies in shock. Recognition of the ineffectiveness of sanctions was widely accepted within the EU in the late 2000s. In 2009, an internal evaluation of the effects of sanctions prepared in the European Commission revealed that they had only been successful technically (i.e. implemented correctly), but not practically or politically.[30]

Sanctions also constrained the EU's role in Myanmar and eventually pushed the latter into Chinese arms. As one author wondered about possible scenarios for Myanmar back in early 2011: "In one, Western sanctions stay in place, and they reduce the influence of Western democracies to near zero".[31] Despite these flaws, the Union had no sound exit strategy and, due to pressure of public expectations and differing views among EU Member States, sanctions would have to be continued indefinitely.[32]

Even though India pursued a more accommodative policy towards Myanmar in the last two decades, it was not any more successful. In the end, this "middle path," or "velvet policy" of soft stance on the military junta and muted support for pro-democracy forces continued to disappoint India and the European Union both within Myanmar and the international community at large, without achieving national objectives.

After almost two decades of engagement of the military junta, Myanmar is more of a land barrier than a land bridge to Southeast Asia; insurgency in the Northeast is simmering with many groups taking shelter behind the border; gas from Myanmar will shortly flow to Chinese Yunnan province instead of India; and China's influence in the country is as strong as ever. Even though India emerged as the fourth largest trade partner of Myanmar, the volume of trade is insignificant and lags far behind that of China. Similarly, Indian investments in Myanmar are minimal,[33] and its development agenda "remains low key and underfunded".[34] In short, "despite this friendly policy, the relationship has not profited India as much as it had hoped".[35]

Cooperation with suspicious Myanmar generals also constrained Indian policy options and came at no costs to the aspiring global power. Since 1992, New Delhi was faced with "the moral dilemma" of choosing between adherence to high ethical standards and principles of *realpolitik* and tried to pursue a "middle path" in its rapprochement with Myanmar military rulers.[36] Despite the continuation of this policy, its effectiveness was hampered by the lack of a common long-term vision and a clear strategy among different Indian ministries, security agencies and politicians. As Renaud Egreteau pointed out in 2011, "an array of contending agendas in New Delhi impede a well-structured and sustainable India–Burma partnership".[37] It has also tarnished India's image both internationally and among large sections of Myanmar society. This was acknowledged by Aung San Suu Kyi during her visit to New Delhi in 2012 when she felt "saddened to feel that we had drawn away from India, or rather that India had drawn away from us, during our difficult days".[38]

Political reforms in Myanmar were received with hope and relief in Europe, and to a lesser extent of the same in India. After careful monitoring and analysis of internal reforms of the President Thein Sein government in 2011 and despite the remaining distrust, the EU tested waters in several visits of European officials to Myanmar in 2011 and eventually started easing sanctions in early 2012. As a first step, on 23 January 2012 the Council of the EU decided to suspend the travel ban (visa restrictions) for several high-level officials from Myanmar, including the President, the Vice-Presidents, Cabinet Members and Speakers of the Houses of Parliament.[39] From 12-14 February the European Commissioner for Development, Andris Piebalgs, paid a visit to Myanmar as the first high-level EU official and announced an additional €150 million in development assistance for 2012-2013, primarily to be spent for health, education, agriculture and the rehabilitation of displaced people in ethnic areas. Brussels deployed a small team of observers in the Myanmar by-elections held on 1 April 2012 at the invitation of the Myanmar government. In April, a traditionally critical European Parliament applauded the fair by-elections in Myanmar and gave a green light for a cautious easing of sanctions.[40]

On 23 April 2012, the EU General Foreign Affairs Council eventually agreed to suspend for one year all sanctions, except for the arms embargo.[41] The EU High Representative Catherine Ashton visited the country from 28-30 April 2012 "to open a new chapter in relations".[42] During the visit, she met with President Thein Sein and Opposition leader Aung San Suu Kyi and inaugurated the EU Office in Yangon. In September, the European Commission initiated procedures "to bring the country back under the so-called 'Everything But Arms' preferential trade regime which would grant duty-free and quota-free access to the European market for all products except for arms and ammunitions".[43]

Once the Union's major political objectives had been attained (release of political prisoners including Aung San Suu Kyi and launch of democratic reforms), Brussels started paying more attention to ethnic reconciliation and peace. Several European officials and politicians expressed concerns and called for the end of ethnic violence in Rakhine state and elsewhere in Myanmar in June and October 2012 and March 2013. In November 2012, President of the European Commission Jose Manuel Barroso visited Myanmar to pledge additional support for the peace process, including funding of the newly established Myanmar Peace Centre (MPC) in Yangon for the same purpose.[44] Political dialogue continued on February 6, 2013 during the visit of Myanmar Foreign Minister Wunna Maung Lwin to Brussels—the first visit by a high-level official from Myanmar in decades.

Myanmar President Thein Sein arrived in Brussels for a historic visit from 5-6 March 2013.[45] In the Joint Statement, both sides pledged to "work in partnership" to "make Myanmar into a modern democracy", "achieve a lasting peace" and "promote human rights and the rule of law". It was also agreed to form a Joint Task Force, which will would meet in Myanmar in November "to assess progress and develop further cooperation in the future".[46] In April 2013, the EU lifted all sanctions on Myanmar except for the arms embargo.[47]

For India, the change in Myanmar did not mean a historical breakthrough like in the case of the EU; it only minimised the constraints of the "moral dilemma" in Indian policy and paved the way for the intensification of bilateral contacts. External Affairs Minister S.M. Krishna paid a visit to Nay Pyi Taw from 20-22 June 2011 as one of first foreign top diplomats to meet the new civilian government. In October Myanmar's new President U Thein Sein led a large delegation, including Chief of General Staff Lt. Gen Hla Htay Win and several ministers for a State visit to New Delhi. Prime Minister Manmohan Singh applauded the on-going transformation in Myanmar and offered "all necessary assistance in further strengthening this democratic transition in an inclusive and broad-based manner" including sharing of India's own experiences "in evolving parliamentary rules, procedures and practices".[48] Both leaders discussed the on-going cooperation in security, infrastructure projects, investments Indian aid, etc. The follow-up of these talks was the visit of a delegation of Myanmar Parliamentarians headed by the Speaker of Lower House (Pyithu Hluttaw) to Delhi in December 2011. In January 2012, Myanmar Foreign Affairs Minister Maung Lwin was again in New Delhi for bilateral talks.

One month after the visit of the EU High Representative to Myanmar, the Indian Prime Minister led a large Indian delegation of several Union Ministers and business leaders from 27-29 May 2012. It was the first visit of an Indian Prime Minister to Myanmar after 25 years and was viewed by many as opening a new chapter in bilateral relations. Both sides discussed closer cooperation in areas like border-area development, transportation, connectivity, agriculture, power and energy, trade and investment, the promotion of friendly exchanges and human resource development. Overall, 12 agreements were signed, including the extension of a new Indian line of credit for US$500 million for Myanmar, several Indian development projects and air services. New Delhi reiterated its readiness to offer "assistance in accelerating the country's democratic transition and developing the capacity of democratic institutions such as the Parliament, National Human Rights Commission and the media" and more precisely to "undertake training programmes for Myanmar Parliamentarians and staff".[49] Both sides committed to improving cooperation on transport infrastructure projects and set 2016 as the deadline for the completion of the Trilateral Highway between India-Myanmar-Thailand.

The intensive dialogue was continued by the exchange of a number of visits: the visit of External Affairs Minister Salman Khurshid to Myanmar from 14-16 December, 2012; that of Myanmar President Thein Sein to Delhi for the India–ASEAN Summit on 22 December 2012; the visit of Speaker of Indian Parliament Meira Kumar to Myanmar in January 2013, along with several exchanges between the military from both sides. Prospects for strengthening of bilateral relations were also discussed during the visit of Aung Sung Suu Kyi to New Delhi from 11-15 November 2012.

Since 2011, India–Myanmar relations gained momentum and New Delhi began to see growing opportunities in Myanmar's opening to the world. In fact, India is "the first to benefit from positive developments within Myanmar and should create the necessary conditions for its "Look East" policy to succeed".[50] One can therefore expect intensified engagement from Indian politicians, military and business in Myanmar and strengthened cooperation in development, infrastructure, energy, counter-insurgency and capacity building. With the decision of the Myanmar government to counterbalance China's influence in the country, more Indian presence in the country would be most welcome.

Working Together for Conflict Resolution in Myanmar?

After two decades of disagreements, the EU and India are apparently on the same page regarding Myanmar. Both sides envisage greater opportunities in the country's democratic transition and offer political and economic support in the process. Lifting of EU sanctions and growing European engagement with the Myanmar government has already removed an important irritant in EU–India relations and will help to improve the strategic partnership. Past disagreements must be left behind and both sides should focus on the future. India has important national interests in Myanmar but often lacks resources to implement its policies in the country. The EU is not a major player in Myanmar but wants to become one. A stable, democratic and fast developing Myanmar will provide more opportunities for both EU and India to attain their national aims.

A crucial area where both partners can explore the potential for joint action is support for the peace process and reconciliation. The simmering ethnic conflict and raising ethnic tensions are indeed the most important current challenges that can still derail the democratic transformation and impede development of the country. Myanmar is a highly diversified society with a difficult history of over six decades of civil wars with numerous ethnic groups. Although no census has made since the colonial times, it is estimated that ethnic Burmans constitute around 68 per cent of the total population, while other major groups include: Shan 9 per cent, Karen 7 per cent, Rakhine 4 per cent, Chinese 3 per cent, Indian 2 per cent, Mon 2 per cent, and others 5 per cent.[51] This is further complicated by many religious minorities. According to the *CIA World Factbook*, 89 per cent of Myanmarese population are Buddhists, 4 per cent Christians (Baptists 3 per cent, Roman Catholics 1 per cent), 4 per cent Muslims, 1 per cent Animist, and the rest constitute 2 per cent. Minorities are located mostly in frontier areas—mountainous and hardly accessible—while Burmans live in the central mainland.

An armed struggle with the ethnic groups started almost on the first day of Myanmar's independence in 1948 and the problem is still far from being resolved. From 1989 to 1996, the government agreed to ceasefires with seventeen major groups, but these broke down in 2010 after they refused to join the Border Guard Forces without the addressing of their political concerns by the military government. Finding a long-lasting solution to the ethnic problem was made a top national priority by the new President, Thein Sein, who in March 2011 offered dialogue with all armed groups without key preconditions.[52] Although some of them agreed to new ceasefire agreements by the end of 2011, the largest ethnic group, viz. the Kachin Independence Organization (KIO), resumed fighting in June 2011. Moreover, ethnic riots against Rohingya Muslims in Rakhine State in June and October 2012 have further exposed the challenge of ethnic relations to national stability and prosperity. Finally, in December 2012 and January 2013 fighting between the military and the Kachin Independence Organization has intensified, posing the risk of an impending new humanitarian crisis. Only after a Chinese intervention was a fragile ceasefire deal reached on 30 May 2013.[53] Still, even though a tentative peace has been reached, the long-term political and economic solution is pending. As was observed in a report of the International Crisis Group: "Once peace agreements are reached, there is an important role for donor countries in providing development assistance and peace-building support to these areas".[54] This naturally opens the door for India and the EU to get involved.

The European Union, as the world's largest donor of development assistance with rich experience in conflict resolution and post-conflict reconstruction in many parts of the world and India with its expertise as functioning multi-ethnic democracy and with good contacts with Myanmar's security establishment, offer complementary assets to assist Myanmar in this difficult period. The European Union has already pledged financial support for the Myanmar Peace Centre in Yangon, €30 million for the peace process and plans to prioritise assistance for this sector in its next Multiannual Programme for 2014-2020. In the EU view, democracy in Myanmar cannot succeed without putting an end to ethnic conflicts. At the same time, it was observed that "focus on peace and conflict resolution, rather than merely human rights, democracy and development could also be promoted by India".[55]

India needs a stable and peaceful Myanmar to realise most of its interests in the region. Though the main areas of insurgency are located along the Chinese border (where the KIO is based) and along the Thai border (where the Karen National Union is based) some armed groups, like the Chin, are located along the Indian border. Moreover, if it wants to construct major transport corridors via Myanmar it would face problems in other unstable areas. As many of Myanmar's ethnic conflicts are cross-border in character, they may need a coordinated regional response. India has indeed been cooperating with Myanmar in countering insurgency along the border since the mid-1990s, and just recently has offered training for military personnel in India as well as support in strengthening democratic institutions and norms. "Multi-ethnic, multi-lingual and multi-religious Myanmar", it is rightly pointed out, "can only achieve genuine national unity and reconciliation by embracing its diversity".[56] India, with its idea of "unity in diversity" and working federal system, seems to have interesting lessons to share with its neighbour.

Although both India and the EU often prefer to work directly with Myanmar, there is much more they can do together in supporting a political solution to ethnic grievances, enhancing inclusive development in ethnic areas or empowering state capacities in enforcing law and order. Some ideas for joint actions include facilitating dialogue on constitutional changes, which can accommodate ethnic aspirations for autonomy without undermining territorial integrity of the state, reforming electoral laws, or training of police and security personnel. The largest potential however lies in cooperation in development assistance in border regions.

After decades of negligence and violence, there is a severe need to build up a peace economy in ethnic areas and provide real benefits for the local population. An improvement of roads, railways, waterways, etc. in Myanmar will have a crucial impact for the country's growth and development. In fact, the realisation of some investments in Myanmar proposed by India would well serve Myanmar's interests and help to establish it as a transport and transit hub in Asia. These include especially the Trilateral Highway from India to Thailand through Myanmar; the road from India to China (the old Stilwell Road) or Kanmodal Multimodal Transport Project from India's Northeast to Myanmar's sea port in Sittwe. The EU and India should discuss ways to co-finance these initiatives in order to secure their fast implementation. This can be done through trilateral development cooperation or through financial institutions like the European Investment Bank or the Asian Development Bank. The EU and India can also discuss ways for trilateral development cooperation with Myanmar in soft projects aimed at strengthening human capital (education, vocational training, health, etc.).

Although there is considerable potential for Europe–India cooperation in Myanmar, there is no guarantee it will be properly exploited. The lesson from Afghanistan, where the two have hardly collaborated in security and development of the country, despite convergence of crucial strategic and economic interests, is not encouraging. Experiences from support for democratic changes or economic development in other South Asian countries (Nepal, Bangladesh) are rather limited. Whether Myanmar will turn out to be another missed opportunity for closer cooperation between India and the EU is yet to be seen in coming years. At present, it offers both entities a historic chance to prove there is substance in their strategic partnership. The next EU–India summit offers the best moment to launch serious talks about engagement in conflict resolution and development in Myanmar and contemplate a more coordinated response.

Notes

1. 96/635/CFSP: Common Position defined by the Council on the basis of Article J.2 of the Treaty on European Union, on Burma/Myanmar, 28 October 1996.
2. "EU Bilateral Trade and Trade with the World: Myanmar," DG Trade, European Commission, 2012.
3. Jared Bissinger, "Foreign Investment in Myanmar: A Resource Boom but a Development Bust?", *Contemporary Southeast Asia*, 34(1), 2012, p. 38. One important exemption to the EU ban on investments in Myanmar is that it does not include companies which established their operations there before the Common Position was agreed on in late 1996. This allows, for instance, a French oil company Total to operate off-shore gas field and gas pipeline to Thailand.
4. European Commission, *The EC Burma/Myanmar Strategy Paper, (2007-2013).*
5. Priyabhala Singh, "India-Myanmar Relations: Strengthening Ties", *World Focus*, no. 396, December 2012, p. 82.

6. Pradip Saikia, "North-East India as a Factor in India's Diplomatic Engagement with Myanmar: Issues and Challenges," *Strategic Analysis*, 33(6), 2009, p. 878.
7. K. Yhome, "India–Myanmar Relations (1998-2008): A Decade of Redefining Bilateral Ties," *ORF Occasional Paper* No. 10, January 2009, p. 3.
8. Bibhu Prasad Routray, "India-Myanmar Relations: Triumph of Pragmatism," *Jindal Journal of International Affairs*, 1(1), October 2011, p. 299.
9. Joint Statement during the visit of Chairman, State Peace and Development Council of Myanmar, New Delhi 27 July 2010.
10. Renaud Egreteau, "A Passage to Burma? India, Development, and Democratization in Myanmar," *Contemporary Politics*, 17(4), 2011, pp. 467-486.
11. Remarks by the President to the Joint Session of the Indian Parliament in New Delhi, 8 November 2010.
12. Renaud Egretau, "Intra-European Bargaining and the 'Tower of Babel' EU Approach to the Burmese Conundrum," *East Asia*, 27(15-33), 2011, p. 23.
13. Sanjib Baruah, "Sweden Probes if India 'Supplied' Arms to Myanmar," *Hindustan Times* (New Delhi), 16 December 2012.
14. Ardeth Maung Thawnghmung and Paul Sarno, "Myanmar Impasses: Alternatives to Isolation and Engagement?", *Asian Journal of Political Science*, 14(1), September 2006, p. 58.
15. P7_TA(2010)0196, European Parliament resolution on the situation in Burma/Myanmar, 20 May 2010.
16. P6_TA(2008)0455, European Parliament resolution on the preparation of the EU–India Summit, 24 September 2008 (Marseilles, 29 September 2008).
17. Indrani Bagchi, "US, EU Want India to Put Pressure on Myanmar," *Times of India*, 28 September 2007.
18. Indrani Bagchi, "Pressure Myanmar: UK Tells India," *Times of India*, 17 October 2007.
19. EU–India Joint Communique, EU–India Summit, Marseilles, 29 September 2008.
20. Population of Overseas Indians, Ministry of Overseas Indian Affairs, Government of India, Ministry website: http://moia.gov.in/index.aspx (last accessed 12 June 2013).
21. Michael Aung Twin, "Parochial Universalism, Democracy Jihad and the Orientalist Image of Burma: The New Evangelism," *Pacific Affairs*, 74(4), Winter 2001-2002, pp. 483-506.
22. Arvind Gupta, "Myanmar's Critical Role in Bolstering India's Look East Policy," IDSA Comment, 2 February 2012.
23. See Pradip Saikia, "North-East India as a Factor in India's Diplomatic Engagement with Myanmar: Issues and Challenges," *Strategic Analysis*, 33(6), (2009), p. 878.
24. Udai Bhanu Singh and Shruti Pandalai, "Myanmar: The Need for Infrastructure Integration," in Rumel Dahiya and Ashok K. Behuria, eds., *India's Neighbourhood: Challenges in the Next Two Decades* (New Delhi: Pentagon Security International, 2012), pp. 110-136.
25. Marie Lall, "Indo-Myanmar Relations in the Era of Pipeline Diplomacy," *Contemporary Southeast Asia*, 28(3), December 2006, pp. 424-446.
26. Yhome, n. 7, p. 9.
27. J. Mohan Malik, "Sino-Indian Rivalry in Myanmar: Implications for Regional

Security," *Contemporary Southeast Asia*, 16(2), September 1994, p. 147.
28. Renaud Egreteau, "Intra-European Bargaining and the 'Tower of Babel' EU Approach to the Burmese Connundrum," *East Asia*, 27(1), 2010, p. 16.
29. Udai Bhanu Singh, "Do the Changes in Myanmar Signify a Real Transition?", *Strategic Analysis*, 37(1), , 2013, p 101.
30. Discussion with an EU official in Warsaw, September 2009.
31. Thant Myint-U, *Where China Meets India: Burma and the New Crossroads of Asia* (London: Faber and Faber, 2011), p. 325.
32. Regreteau, n. 28, p. 18.
33. According to one estimate, "While investment from many other countries has risen and fallen, FDI from India seems to have never started. From 1988 until March 2009, actual FDI from India totalled only $200,000, much smaller than the $175 million of investment approvals." See Bissinger, n. 3, p. 38.
34. Egreteau, n. 10, p. 479.
35. Renaud Egreteau, "India's Ambitions in Burma: More Frustration than Success? "*Asian Survey*, 48(6), November/December2008, pp. 936-957.
36. Syed Ali Mujtaba, "India–Myanmar Relations: Predicament and Prospects," in K. Raja Reddy, ed., *Foreign Policy of India and Asia-Pacific* (New Delhi: New Century Publications, 2012).
37. Egreteau, n. 10, p. 481.
38. "Burma's Aung San Suu Kyi Appeals for India Support", BBC, New Delhi, 14 November 2012.
39. Press Release, 3142nd Council meeting, Foreign Affairs, Brussels, 23 January 2012.
40. European Parliament Resolution on the Situation in Burma/Myanmar, Strasbourg, 20 April 2012.
41. Press Release, 3159th Foreign Affairs Council meeting, Brussels, 23 April 2012.
42. Press Release, "Catherine Ashton Visits Burma/Myanmar to Open a New Chapter in the Relationship", Brussels, 27 April 2012.
43. Press Release, "European Commission Proposes to Reinstate Trade Preferences to Myanmar/Burma", Brussels, 17 September 2012.
44. Press Release, "EC President Jose Manuel Barroso, Minister Aung Min Sign Joint Declaration at Myanmar Peace Centre", Brussels, 3 November 2012.
45. Statement by the spokesperson of EU High Representative Catherine Ashton following the meeting with the Foreign Minister of Myanmar, U Wunna Maung Lwin, Brussels, 6 February 2013.
46. Joint Statement, "Building a Lasting EU–Myanmar Partnership", Brussels, 5 March 2013.
47. Council Conclusions on Myanmar/Burma, 3236th Foreign Affairs Council meeting, Luxembourg, 22 April 2013
48. Joint Statement on the occasion of the visit of President of the Republic of the Union of Myanmar U Thein Sein to India, New Delhi, 14 October 2011.
49. Joint Statement on the occasion of the State Visit of Prime Minister of the Republic of India, Dr. Manmohan Singh to the Republic of the Union of Myanmar, Nay Pyi Taw, 28 May 2012.
50. Namrata Goswami,"Look East for New Friends," *The Times of India*, 9 December 2012.
51. *CIA World Factbook* available at https://www.cia.gov/library/publications/the-world-factbook/ (accessed on 12 June 2013).

52. See *Myanmar: A New Peace Initiative*, Crisis Group Asia Report No. 214, 30 November 2011.
53. *A Tentative Peace in Myanmar's Kachin Conflict*, Crisis Group Asia Briefing No.140, 12 June 2013.
54. *Myanmar: A New Peace Initiative*, n. 52, p. ii.
55. Egreteau, n. 10, p. 483.
56. *Myanmar: A New Peace Initiative*, n. 52.

Index